DEEPER STILL

Books by Edna Ellison

available from New Hope Publishers

The "Friend to Friend" series

Friendships of Purpose: A Shared Study of Ephesians

Friendships of Faith: A Shared Study of Hebrews

Friend to Friend: Enriching Friendships
Through a Shared Study of Philippians

Woman to Woman: Preparing Yourself to Mentor
Coauthored by Tricia Scribner

Seeking Wisdom: Preparing Yourself to Be Mentored
Coauthored by Tricia Scribner

DEEPER STILL

A Woman's Study
to a Closer Walk with God

By Edna Ellison

new
hope
PUBLISHERS

Birmingham, Alabama

New Hope® Publishers
P. O. Box 12065
Birmingham, AL 35202-2065
www.newhopepublishers.com

Library of Congress Cataloging-in-Publication Data

Ellison, Edna.
  Deeper still : a woman's study to a closer walk with God / by Edna Ellison.
    p. cm.
  ISBN 1-59669-013-5 (softcover)
  1. Christian women—Religious life. 2. Spirituality. 3. Spiritual formation. I. Title.
  BV4527.E455 2006
  248.8'43—dc22
            2006008134

ISBN: 1-59669-013-5

N064146 • 0806 • 4M1

Dedication

To my family: Blakely Joy Ellison, the joy of all our family; her talented mother, Wendy, my dear daughter-in-love; my son Jack, my firstborn and well-loved, now-adult child; Patsy Farmer, my youngest, who will be my precious baby even when she's forty-one; and the Right Reverend Timothy Farmer, my son-in-love, a quiet, stable presence in our lives. Each one of these has enriched me in more ways than I can name.

TABLE OF CONTENTS

———————●———————

ACKNOWLEDGMENTS

───────────── ● ─────────────

This book has been a joy to write, but I could not have written it without the help of many wonderful people. I have been blessed to have the talented staff at New Hope Publishers as colleagues. Andrea Mullins, publisher, has led the company as a godly Christian woman of purpose and faith. Thank you, Andrea, for believing in me and trusting my work. You have been a great encourager. Rebecca England has served as a patient, professional editor who has great knowledge of her craft as well as depth of Christian understanding and guidance. Thank you, Rebecca, for all you mean to me as a continuing editor through five books. You have helped make these words come alive. I am indebted also to Jean Baswell, copy editor, for a willing spirit and careful attention to this project, along with Wendy Wakefield and Tina Atchenson for the completion of the printing and marketing.

I also appreciate the patience of my family, who stood by me while I planned layout pages, researched, outlined, typed, and revised again and again on the computer, polishing the pages of this work. Thank you, Patsy and Tim, for understanding as I lived like a Bohemian hermit for several days at a time during spurts of creativity. Thanks for sharing your electronic router and for sharing your home with my office as I write every day. A sincere thank you also goes to Jack and Wendy for a lap pad for my hot laptop, which brings comfort and blessings as I write. Thank you, dear Blakely, my only granddaughter; you give me joy and inspiration for the days of pouring out my spirit onto paper. Nothing is better during a heavy writing schedule than to hear your voice on the phone: "I love you, Mimi! See you soon!"

I owe thanks to my Aunt Alice, who gave me editorial advice on my writing in general and who inspired me often with wise words. Thank you, also, Women by Design, who have encouraged me: Tricia Scribner, my dear *merea*; Kimberly Sowell, my speaking manager; Marie Alston, Cherie Nettles, and Joy Brown.

I especially thank God who has led me every step of the way, from the first attempt at an outline to the completion of the last page through the final edit. As Paul says, we are only His servants, always content, and honored to contribute and serve in the smallest way. I am grateful to Him who is the beginning of all wisdom and the One who leads us all deeper and deeper still into His heart.

INTRODUCTION

•

Portrait of a Deeper-Still Christian

Are you a deeper-still Christian? If you are avidly in progress in acquiring wisdom and holiness; if you live each day in the *becoming* as well as the *doing* of the Christian life; if you are earnestly, seriously serving Jesus; and if you already know the basics of Christianity and are plunging into a deeper step, opening your heart—deeper and deeper still—to the work of the Holy Spirit; yet you realize you're not *spiritually mature*, but *spiritually maturing*…then this book is for you.

Perhaps you have read many Christian how-to books that failed to address your needs. They seemed to provide surface answers to a maturing Christian's deeper-than-surface living. Jesus said, "Be perfect, therefore, as your heavenly Father is perfect" (Matthew 5:48). Yet no matter how mature you become in Christ, you realize you can't reach the goal of perfection in your lifetime. You'll find perfection (or *completeness*) only in the place of perfection, completed by the God of perfection, in heaven. Paul says, "For we know in part…but when perfection comes, the imperfect disappears…. Now I know in part; then I shall know fully, even as I am fully known" (1 Corinthians 13:9, 10, 12).

Why should you strive in the dark for spiritual maturity, if it's impossible to attain and the quest for it is endless? The answer is simple: Something compels you! *You hunger for the gospel.* The writer of Hebrews urges: "Let us throw off everything that hinders and the sin that so easily entangles, and let us run with perseverance the race marked out for us. Let us fix our eyes on Jesus, the author and perfecter of our faith, who for the joy set before him endured the cross…so that you will not grow weary and lose heart" (Hebrews 12:1–3).

Paul also admits he's not perfect, yet he says he's compelled to move toward the perfection in heaven:

> *Not that I have already obtained all this, or have already been made perfect, but I press on to take hold of that for which Christ Jesus took hold of me. Brothers, I do not consider myself yet to have taken hold of it. But one thing I do: Forgetting what is behind and straining toward what is ahead, I press on toward the goal to win the prize for which God has called me heavenward in Christ Jesus…. Our citizenship is in heaven. And we eagerly await a Savior from there, the Lord Jesus Christ. (Philippians 3:12–14, 20)*

You go to church every time the church doors are open, because you don't want to miss any chance to hear the Lord speak— to gain more knowledge—*deeper still*, in the mystery of the divine. You expect to worship Him as His Spirit comes down and fills your

14

church each time you attend. You hunger for the testimonies and training by more mature Christians in your church, who can share with you the deeper-still secrets of their mysterious passion to do things that the world would consider sacrifice beyond sanity! You serve with your Christian friends in many arenas of service, because you have a compelling passion to serve others. You pray for hundreds—no, *thousands*—of opportunities to do *more* ministry, deeper still, to change the world. When you think of Christ's sacrifice for you, your enthusiasm and compassion increases, and you can hardly sit still when you think of all the challenging work He *might* allow you to do for Him. You eagerly await His call, hoping for the chance to serve Him, live wisely, and grow spiritually as His mature servant, deeper still, at His feet.

What is the desire of your heart? Do you eagerly look for missions and ministries? Do you earnestly pray for your heart to be involved in worship that is deeper still? Are you avidly practicing the spiritual disciplines of daily Bible study and prayer—not perfectly, but consistently? If this is the desire of your heart, then this book is for you.

So who should read this book? Anyone who feels you are spiritually mature, if you are seeking God's direction for the next exciting step. Anyone who does not feel spiritually mature, but you know you are touched by the mystery of Jesus Christ, and you want to grow toward heaven's perfection. Anyone who doesn't understand the mystery at all and stands on square one looking for square two. Christian maturity is not for the elite. It is for everyone. It's for you.

How should you read this book? Pray first. Seek out the mysteries as you communicate with your personal Savior who cares about every part of your life. Read God's Word found in this Bible study and pray the Scriptures daily. (You'll find more information on prayer in study 5.) Then meditate on what you've discovered to feed your passion for serving Him.

Each day's study will contain three special features:
1. **Questions** for further thought or discussion on the topic for the day
2. **M&M: Ministry and Missions Moment**, in which you can delve deeper into God's Word as a step toward spiritual discipline and maturity
3. **Deeper Still: Mystery Revealed**, a spiritual principle you can put to practice in your everyday life

My prayer for you is that this series of Bible study books will lead you into spiritual depth and that you will discover you are a leadership of one, as God makes you *willing and able to do the unbelievable* in Christ's power. I pray that you can be the perfect portrait of a *deeper-still Christian*, avidly seeking progress in your quest to grow closer to Him, to delve into His truths, eager to become a mentor and a leader in the Great Commandment and the Great Commission. I hope this book study will lead you to a growth spurt in wisdom and holiness! "My purpose is that they may be encouraged in heart and united in love, so that they may have the full riches of complete understanding, in order that they may know the *mystery* of God, namely, Christ, in whom are hidden all the *treasures of wisdom and knowledge*" (Colossians 2:2–3, italics added). God bless you in special ways as you discover Him in this Bible study book.

Unit 1

---•---

CHARACTERISTICS OF SPIRITUAL MATURITY

A Holy God came down from heaven, deeper, deeper still;
Lower than the angels Jesus came, with holiness.

Somehow perfect, holy Love came tumbling in our hearts,
Making them ring true and pure, pouring forth, O Lord,

A sudden rush of wisdom seen only by His own,
Who journey to the heart of God, go deeper, deeper still.

The Presence of Your Spirit, Lord, awakes in us anew,
And helps us dare to pray courageous words You hear, I know.

——— Study 1 ———
Holy, Wholly Holey

The night of the musical, during a short snack break, I saw my son, Jack, who'd been practicing all afternoon with the youth choir. "Hey," he said, looking at my new blue velvet skirt. "Lookin' good!"

"Thanks," I said, surprised. "What do you want?" (No 14-year-old son gives his mother a compliment without an ulterior motive.) "I do need a favor, Mom. I left my good shoes at home. These old tennis shoes don't match my suit…gotta get those shoes!" I'd already eaten, so I left quickly to pick up the shoes (a few blocks away) while he enjoyed the youth snacks.

Driving home, I practiced the women's trio alto part for "Holy, Holy, Holy." I sang it until I was satisfied my pitch was perfect. Looking into the car mirror, I practiced my holiest facial expressions. Then I looked down at the blue skirt. *You even look holy,* I said to myself, stroking the beautiful velvet fabric, which I'd cut and sewn myself. I felt even holier because my hands had created the beautiful outfit. I was really going to be "lookin' good"—singing a holy song, looking superholy in that velvet skirt!

It was dark by the time I got home. I ran through the darkened carport toward the kitchen door. Suddenly I stumbled over Jack's dirt bike, propped up on a cement block for repair. Falling over the motorcycle, I made a three-point landing with my knees on the block and my chin on the bottom step at the back door. The rough brick step scratched my chin. I ran quickly inside, grabbed Jack's shoes, checked my watch, and then looked in the mirror. My chin was bleeding! I pressed a clean wet washcloth against it, knowing

Deeper Still

the bleeding would stop in a few minutes. At the last minute, I grabbed a bottle of foundation makeup to cover the spot and ran out the door.

On the way to the church the bleeding stopped, I relaxed, and then I noticed my skirt: right in the middle of the front was an L-shaped tear about two inches in each direction! I arrived at the church disheveled and out of breath. "What will I do?" I said to the other women in the trio, after I'd given the shoes to Jack. They grabbed the makeup and dabbed it over the red scratch on my chin. Then they turned the skirt back to front so that the tear would not be noticeable—at least not to anybody in the congregation. The choir was all smiles when I stepped out to the microphones as my legs showed through the velvet skirt. After the trio's song, I backed up stiffly without turning and sat down on the second row in the choir loft. Afterward, one of the men grinning in the choir said, "Edna, as you sang 'Holy, Holy, Holy,' you were wholly holey!"

Do you remember a time when your perfect façade was shot with holes, as Edna's was? Share the incident with a study partner or friend if you feel comfortable doing so.

What's the difference in being *holy* and *wholly holey*?

Define holiness in your own words:

How do people get holy?

Is holiness a prerequisite for going to heaven?

Becoming Who You Are

Since then, I've realized his remark is true: most of us sing about holiness, but we have holes in our souls. You might say we are wholly holey. We say proper words and hold our mouths just right in church to sound and look holy, but the truth is we'll never be completely holy until we get to heaven. (See Portrait of a Deeper-Still Christian in the Introduction.) Our only holiness comes from accepting Christ in our hearts. No good works can ever bring us holiness; but as He, the Most Holy One, lives inside our spirits, we become more like Him.

The Bible compares God's holy people—that is, those *sanctified*, or *made holy* through Him—with the world: the holy ones are mature; the unholy ones are immature (amateurs in the faith), or babes in Christ. "You are a chosen people, a royal priesthood, a *holy* nation, a people belonging to God, that you may declare the praises of him who called you out of darkness into his wonderful light" (1 Peter 2:9, italics added). As a Christian, *holy* describes you. "You shall be holy, for I the LORD your God am holy" (Leviticus 19:2 NKJV). *Holy* is who we are as the people of God. Inside us, because we are God's people, wells up a yearning to become *who we are*! Sometimes we feel awkward, embarrassed, or incomplete if we have accepted Christ but have never grown in our spiritual maturity and accepted His holiness set before us.

At times, we fail to see our holiness even when it is offered. It's a mysterious thing hidden in the darkness. I stumbled over Jack's motorcycle in the dark. However, the darkness began in my car, even before I got to the house. It began with my pride, as I looked in the mirror; practiced "looking holy"; listened to the sound of my own voice mouthing "Holy, Holy, Holy"; and took pride in *my* handmade skirt. I knew I was "lookin' good"! I hadn't focused on singing praise to God; I'd concentrated on my perfect sound, my perfect look, my perfect family—*my* everything. I had missed the mark of holiness completely. I stumbled and fell spiritually as well as physically that night. The writer of Hebrews tells me why I missed the mark:

> *You are slow to learn. In fact, though by this time you ought to be teachers, you need someone to teach you the elementary truths of God's word all over again. You need milk, not solid food! Anyone who lives on milk, being still an infant, is not acquainted with the teaching about righteousness. But solid food is for the mature, who by constant use have trained themselves to distinguish good from evil. (Hebrews 5:11–14)*

Try this exercise: underline the important phrases in the passage above, starting with the last sentence in verse 14 and working backward to the first one in verse 11.

In the 1980s, I visited The Church of the Saviour in Washington, DC. The pastor, Dr. Newton Gordon Cosby, said these words: "Let go the surface; journey in the deeps." He also asked us to let go of the things that prevented us from diving into God's deepest heart, and challenged us to dive in!

As you work through each study in this book, you will be nearer to *who you are*. Judy King once said, "Most people miss so much of who they are, but the tragedy is that they missed it without realizing they missed it." Don't miss the most important part of life without realizing you missed it.

Finish these significant sentences according to what you read in Hebrews 5:11–14, starting with the last sentence and working backward:

I need to distinguish good from…

I can do this if I…

Solid food is for…

Anyone who lives on milk is…

We get elementary truths from…

We learn elementary truths from…

I ought to be a…

If I'm not a teacher, then I am…

Understanding the Holiness Code

Hebrews 5:14 states the basics of all morality: you need to distinguish good from *evil*. God, the judge of good and evil, has provided His Word to help you distinguish between these two opposites. In Exodus 20:1–17, He provides the Ten Commandments. In Leviticus 11–15, He provides a passage known as "The Holiness Code." In it, God sets forth the elementary laws for holiness, which teach us how to become holy. (The Holiness Code has initiated laws for most of humanity down through the centuries. In fact, this code set the pattern for most Western laws.) This whole Leviticus passage is laws of what is clean and unclean, not the basis for most countries' laws.

To obey God's laws, you distinguish good from evil, according to Hebrews 5:11–14, by *training yourself through constant use in distinguishing between the two.* In other words, you need to discipline yourself, through prayer and Bible study, to practice discerning the difference. Jerome, one of the early fathers of the Christian church, said, "Sanctification comes due to your will and effort." Notice that verse 13 says solid food is for the *mature.* You are mature if you have trained yourself to grow in spiritual maturity. If you have not done this (eaten solid food, disciplining yourself to go *deeper still* into your relationship with God so you'll become spiritually mature), then you live on milk; in short, you are still an *infant, a baby who knows nothing* and is not acquainted with righteous teaching. You get these elemental truths from *God's Word,* the Bible. Just as you learn elementary truths from elementary school teachers, you, as a maturing Christian, learn as much as you can from *a good Bible teacher,* and then you ought to become a *teacher.* If you're not one, you're *slow to learn.*

How do you feel about becoming a teacher? Check all that apply:
- ❏ **I don't want to stand before people with sweaty palms and a dry throat.**
- ❏ **Thanks, but no thanks. I can't do that.**
- ☑ **I think teaching happens at "the teachable moment." Maybe I can.**
- ☑ **God will show me when to speak.**
- ☑ **I can share with others my experience with God or teach several Bible verses I understand.**
- ☑ **I can teach simply, in a comfortable, casual setting, as God leads.**
- ☑ **I know God will empower me if I step out in faith.**

Holiness in the Inner Heart

In the New Testament, God establishes a New Covenant in which He says, "I will put my laws in their minds and write them on their hearts. I will be their God…they will all know me, from the least of them to the greatest" (Hebrews 8:10–11). Good news! God wants you and me—every one of us, not just the elite Christians—to know Him deeper, more personally. How do you do that? By knowing good from evil and choosing good. By practicing holiness. By taking control of your life and disciplining yourself to grow spiritually *more* mature, no matter how mature you believe you are already! John Owen, in "The Holy Spirit," said, "Holiness indeed is perfected in heaven: but the beginning of it is invariably confined to this world."

In spite of the clarification of God's laws in the Old and New Testaments, people have often misunderstood the true nature of spiritual maturity or holiness. They think it's a matter of doing, not becoming. As a *deeper-still* Christian, you must go further, deeper than your first understanding of salvation, in your Christian life. "Therefore, let us leave the elementary teachings about Christ and go on to maturity" (Hebrews 6:1). The writer of Hebrews says he can assume you are already living by the elementary teachings about repentance, salvation, and baptism—and, of course, you will want to continue those teachings—but if you want to become a *deeper-still* Christian, you will not become entangled in external rituals as a means to spiritual maturity. The words of John Charles Ryle, the nineteenth-century "working man's bishop," ring true: "Union with Christ is the root of holiness." Spiritual maturity is a by-product of the working of the Holy Spirit of Christ in your life and your willingness to submit to His spiritual discipline.

M&M: *Ministry and Missions Moment*

When someone suggested I write this book, the first of three in one year, I replied, "I don't have enough wisdom." I was right. I don't have the wisdom, but God has. He wants me to stop leading and let Him work through me to write this Bible study. As He leads, I will be able to do it. (If you are reading the completed book now, you'll know *He* did it.)

Do you have a life verse from the Bible, which you've claimed to guide you till death? A verse for a mission statement of your faith? If not, search for one today. If you do have one, *it could be that God is calling you to step into a new arena of ministry and missions*, such as teaching. If you know only a few verses, start telling someone what God has shown you! Share with a child, neighbor, Sunday School class, or sick friend who needs God's wisdom. While you continue in your spiritual maturing process, this book will suggest steady disciplines, outrageous ministries, and radical missions endeavors you can consider, as God nudges you along the path.

Meditate on Hebrews 5:7–9; Isaiah 42:19–20; 1 Thessalonians 4:7; and 1 Chronicles 16:29. In the categories that follow, write additional ideas that come to mind about stepping out in faith for a *deeper-still* ministry.

God is leading me deeper still. Here are my meditation thoughts on the following:

Practicing, training our senses (eyes and ears) to discern good and evil:

Obedience through suffering:

Holiness:

Deeper Still: *Mystery Revealed*

This is a spiritual principle learned from years of experience: *I know I'm approaching spiritual maturity when I place myself last and God first. When I forget my wisdom and depend on His. When I'm willing to open my mouth and let Him speak. When I quit leading and let Him do it.* It's a matter of *selflessness,* which I seldom achieve. Pray about your spiritual maturing, asking for personal holiness. As you continue maturing, this Bible study will suggest other areas of walking in holiness, continuing in faith along a *deeper-still* way.

—— Study 2 ——

Sincere Love of God

One hot July when I was a preteen, I attended Vacation Bible School at Bush River Baptist Church in Newberry County, South Carolina. We studied Romans 3 and 8 during the week, learned the pledge to the Christian flag, sang "Deep and Wide" and other Christian songs, played baseball in the dusty churchyard at a mid-morning break, and made pincushions for a craft. On the last day, a college ministerial student, our youth pastor for the summer, talked sincerely about God. I don't remember his name, but I'll never forget the sincere love of God I saw in his eyes and the words he said that day: "Edna, you need God." I said nothing, but I thought, *So what? I've known that for years!* My parents had accompanied me to Sunday School and church services all my life. I knew about Almighty God, who created heaven and earth. Sure, we needed Him to provide our daily bread, give us rain and sunshine, and sustain life itself.

Then our youth pastor said something that hit me right between the eyes: "And, Edna, God needs you."

What? I began listening closer. *God needs me?* I thought. *How could that be? Why would the Almighty God, who hung the sun and stars in place, need me?* I left church that day contemplating a new thought: *The Creator God needs me!* My "all-sufficient, gentle-grandfather" image of Almighty God was suddenly blown away! This God wanted me—personally!

That night my mother surprised my brother, Jim, and me by doing something unusual: she let us go to bed without a bath. What fun! I jumped into my bed without the dreaded nightly bath. Moments later, however, the bed felt gritty and uncomfortable. I glanced down at my legs, still dusty from sliding into home plate during the ball game. I realized I was dirty inside and out. In the dark I recalled how mean I'd been that summer: I'd knocked Jim's front teeth out with a baseball—on purpose. I'd also pinched my cousin Lamar's arm until it had blue marks (because he had wanted to play with us older cousins. Humph!). As I reviewed all the naughty things I'd done that summer, I faced my sinful nature for the first time.

Details of that night are as real to me today as they were then: a dog barking in the distance, my mother softly snoring in the next room, the smell of honeysuckle drifting through screens on the open windows…and suddenly I felt the presence of God, tangible love, in my room. I said, "Lord, I don't know what You'd need from a skinny little girl like me. I'm ignorant and dirty—inside and out—but right now I want to give You my heart, with all its sin, which I'm sorry for. Like the guy said today at church, I believe Jesus died for my sins. I can't image how I could ever help You, Lord, but I want to…. I want to give You everything I am now and ever will be. Help me live as a good girl, not a mean one." All of a sudden, I knew I was different, somehow assured, and tremendously happy. He had forgiven me and would be with me always. I knew His love *was* deep and wide—and real.

Oswald Chambers, the great English preacher, wrote his wife, Biddy, that she could never understand God's ways, but he advised: "Get down into his love." Getting *down* is the way to God's love.

God's Example of Love

Jehovah God gave us the perfect example of love at Creation. His Spirit "hovered over the deep," loving the whole earth, as He brought order out of chaos. He still brings order out of chaos in our world: "abounding in love to all who call" (Psalm 86:5). God's abundant love is complete, or perfect, as *it makes you complete*.

Giving you an example of how to love, God loved you with a primal love that is *first* (1 John 4:19), great (Ephesians 2:4), everlasting (Psalm 103:17), tender (Daniel 1:9), merciful (Deuteronomy 7:9), and from which you will never be separated (Romans 8:39). It is a love that fulfills the Old Testament Law (Romans 13:10), covers all your sins (Proverbs 10:12), is demonstrated by His sacrifice for you (Romans 5:8), and surely will flow into your heart (Romans 5:5) when you invite Him inside. From that point on, you are able to abide in His great love (John 15:10). You can be assured God knows you personally (1 Corinthians 8:3)—and because He does, He blesses you and your family in the relationship (Deuteronomy 7:13).

Because God loves you, you don't need to be afraid: He will protect you and be your stronghold against fear (Psalm 27:1–3). God cherishes you. His Word promises that because He loves you, you are worth much—a significant person, even in the world (Isaiah 43:4–5).

Look up the Scriptures in today's study. Pray that God will help you understand them in a personal way. Write your

thoughts about the characteristics of God's love as you have matured:

Your Response to His Love

The significance of this "*first* love" makes love one of the major characteristics of spiritual maturity. When Christ gives blessings and curses on the seven New Testament mission churches, He condemns the one at Ephesus: "I hold this against you: You have forsaken your *first love*" (Revelation 2:4). Early in the Old Testament, God had given His people these words about love, which came to be known as the *Schema*: "Hear, O Israel…Thou shalt love the LORD thy God with all thine heart, and with all thy soul, and with all thy might" (Deuteronomy 6:4–5 KJV). Later, in the New Testament, Jesus said, "Thou shalt love the Lord your God with all thy heart, and with all thy soul, and with all thy mind, and with all thy strength: this is the *first* commandment." (Mark 12:30 KJV). If you have a spiritually maturing heart, you will center your whole being on the first love: God loved you *first*.

❧ Loving with all your heart promotes emotional centeredness.
❧ Loving with all your soul promotes spiritual centeredness.
❧ Loving with all your mind promotes mental, intellectual centeredness.
❧ Loving with all your strength promotes physical centeredness.

However, most people do not achieve this total spiritual centeredness. Studying people and the way they loved, John of Caribou outlined four degrees of love:

1. Love yourself.
2. Love God for selfish reasons.
3. Love yourself for God's sake.
4. Love God for God's sake.

It is only under the fourth degree of love that we can live by the Golden Rule: "Do to others what you would have them do to you" (Matthew 7:12). *When you love God for God's sake, recognizing that He first loved you, growing and remembering your first love, only then can you love others as yourself, the way He did.*

From your own life, give examples of times you use the four degrees of love.

1.

2.

3.

4.

What kind of activities would help you mature in the fourth degree of love?

What is your personal response to His great love?

As you grow in spiritual maturity, God's love urges a response in you:

- ❦ Love salvation (Psalm 40:16).
- ❦ Love His law (Psalm 119:113).
- ❦ Love truth and peace (Zechariah 8:19).
- ❦ Love His precepts (Psalm 119:159).
- ❦ And even love His very name (Psalm 5:11)!

As you further mature in your love, you do the following:

- ❦ Love being spiritually alert as you work daily (Proverbs 20:13).
- ❦ Become quieted by His love as you rely on him daily (Zephaniah 3:17).
- ❦ Love to pray as His Spirit leads daily (Romans 15:30).
- ❦ Love His commands as you study them daily (John 14:15).
- ❦ Love mercy as you walk humbly with Him daily (Micah 6:8).

Loving Him with every facet of your being, you are able to go deeper, still deeper, into His Spirit.

Characteristics of Sincere Love, as God Refines

According to the apostle Paul, as you delve deeper into the Holy Spirit, and as Christ dwells in your heart through faith, He refines that love. You become "rooted and established [or *grounded*, KJV] in love…filled to the measure of all the fullness of God" (Ephesians 3:17, 19). When you are full, you overflow into the lives of others. You are able to do the following:

- ❦ Love others *sincerely* (John 13:34; Romans 12:10).
- ❦ Love your spouse *sincerely* (Ephesians 5:25; Titus 2:4).
- ❦ Love your neighbor *sincerely* as yourself (Matthew 5:43).
- ❦ *Sincerely* love your friends more deeply (John 15:13).
- ❦ Love even your enemies (John 15:44)—*sincerely*!

The mark of spiritually mature Christians, then, is that their love is sincere (2 Corinthians 8:8). In addition, it is

1. energized by faith (Galatians 5:6);
2. discerning, in deeper knowledge and insight (Philippians 1:9);
3. shown to all people, especially in churches (2 Corinthians 8:24);
4. enabling as it helps them to stand united with other Christians in "the same love" (Philippians 2:2), to speak the truth in love (Ephesians 4:15), and to work together in love as the body of Christ, edifying each other (Ephesians 4:16); and
5. motivating, as it stirs them to serve others (Galatians 5:13b), to offer comfort to them (Philippians 2:1), and to do such things as a labor of love (1 Thessalonians 1:3).

Since love is a fruit of the Spirit of God living in you (Galatians 5:22), your love is also patient, kind, persevering, always trusting, always hoping. It has no envy, boasting, rudeness, or prideful self-seeking, as Paul says in 1 Corinthians 13. Love is a way to walk (Ephesians 5:2), accompanying a sound mind (2 Timothy 1:7), and bringing joy and consolation (Philippians 2:1). "And over all these virtues put on love, which binds them all together in perfect unity" (Colossians 3:14).

On a scale of 1 to 10 (10 being the highest), rate yourself in the maturity of your love on each of the following points:

❧ **Sincerity**   1 2 3 4 5 6 7 8 9 10
❧ **Energized by faith**   1 2 3 4 5 6 7 8 9 10
❧ **Discerning**   1 2 3 4 5 6 7 8 9 10
❧ **United with other Christians** 1 2 3 4 5 6 7 8 9 10
❧ **Motivated to serve others**   1 2 3 4 5 6 7 8 9 10
❧ **Patient**   1 2 3 4 5 6 7 8 9 10
❧ **Kind**   1 2 3 4 5 6 7 8 9 10

❦ Persevering   1 2 3 4 5 6 7 8 9 10
❦ Trusting and hoping   1 2 3 4 5 6 7 8 9 10
❦ Nonprideful   1 2 3 4 5 6 7 8 9 10

Rewards for Loving God Sincerely

God makes it clear that your love of Christ will earn rewards: inheriting the kingdom of God (James 2:5) and receiving a crown. Peter says that as you live here on earth, your sincere love will enable you to love life, enjoying every day (1 Peter 3:10). God's abounding love gives the spiritually mature Christian a gift of interdependence, a bond with all people, which we'll discuss in other portions of this book. In heaven and on earth, God's love is truly *made complete in you,* as you sincerely love His Word and walk as Jesus did (1 John 2:5; 4:12).

M&M: *Ministry and Missions Moment*

When God told the Israelites to "love the LORD your God with all your heart, and soul, and strength," He instructed them to write the words on their hearts, to teach them to their children, to speak of them when they sat at home or walked on the road, to wear them as revered symbols on their forehands and hands and to write them on their doorframes and gates (Deuteronomy 6:4–9)—anything to keep them from forgetting their first love. What can you do to help your children, grandchildren, siblings, or extended family to love God? Make Scripture cards to give to family members; share them with hospital or nursing home patients. Consider distributing Scripture portions on a missions trip in America or overseas. Remind others that God loved them first.

Deeper Still: *Mystery Revealed*

Here's the spiritual mystery for today: *the more love you give away, the more you get in return.* Living and walking in God's love causes your love to increase. As it grows, it flows out into the lives of others. Pray that God will enable you to demonstrate your love for Him as you multiply it among others. "How great is the love the Father has lavished on us, that we should be called children of God" (1 John 3:1)!

—— Study 3 ——
A Pure Heart

Everything about God is pure: His love, His motives, His plans for you, His actions.... Human words can't list all the ways God is pure. Everything He says or does arises out of a pure heart. King David said, "The words of the LORD are pure words" (Psalm 12:6 KJV). A few years later, David's son King Solomon said, "The words of the pure are pleasant" (Proverbs 15:26 KJV). If you want to be pure in heart, you must recognize your position in life. God takes you just the way you are, poor or rich, Jew or Gentile, saint or sinner. *If you think you've moved beyond "Just As I Am," you haven't.* The only thing you contribute to your relationship with God is the sin that made His death necessary. If you're spiritually maturing, you'll recognize that whatever your possessions, you are a beggar, standing and shivering before Him, pleading for mercy, thankful for the grace He's given you. You accept that you may even be wellborn, but not born again. Recognizing your position at His feet is the first step toward purity of heart.

If you believe in God, who is pure in heart, you want to follow His example. Anything that comes out of your heart would be pure only as you align yourself with God, find divine intimacy with Him, and see His heart. Jesus said, "Blessed are the pure in heart, for they will see God" (Matthew 5:8).

Characteristics of a Pure Heart

People with pure hearts can be defined by what they are not: they are not deceitful, mean, murderous, envious, immoral, or unfair. We might assume most individuals on Death Row in a federal prison are not pure in heart. Neither are child molesters, sexual abusers, or murderers—whether they are in jail or not. People who are streetwise, rough, or crude are often people of impure hearts, partially because of their experience. On the other hand, those who are naive don't necessarily have a pure heart. People may have knowledge, but it may be about evil things. James says, "Wisdom that comes from heaven is first of all pure" (James 3:17).

Seven specific characteristics are present in a person with a pure heart:

1. A Foundation of Pure Motives

As a maturing Christian, a basic characteristic is that you have pure motives. In other words, without deceit in your heart, seek God with all you have. Love Him with your whole heart, in sincere adoration, with no strings attached. As you interact with others, desire only good for them. Treat them fairly, honestly, out of a pure heart.

2. A Clear Conscience

Job's friends tried to convince him that he and his children had obviously sinned, since they had suffered. Like many mature believers, Job was confident that his heart was "pure and upright." He didn't brag, but he loved the Lord and followed His precepts wholeheartedly. Paul describes such people—those mature Christians qualified to be leaders—in his letter to Timothy: "They must keep hold of the deep truths of the faith with a clear conscience" (1 Timothy 3:9). The psalmist said, "Who may stand in his holy place? He who has clean hands and a pure heart" (Psalm 24:4). As any mature Christian would, Paul gives this advice to young Timothy: "Keep yourself pure" (1 Timothy 5:22). A clean conscience ushers you into the presence of the King of kings, yet the presence of sin is a barrier to your prayers (Psalm 66:18; Isaiah 59:1–2). *If you want to communicate with God and keep the lines open, then "call on the Lord out of a pure heart"* (2 Timothy 2:22).

3. Unselfishness Growing from the Heart

People with a pure heart go a step beyond that innocent motive and clear conscience. They live out deep purity in their interactions with others. "Even a child is known by his actions, by whether his conduct is pure and right" (Proverbs 20:11). The psalmist says to God, "To the pure you show yourself pure" (Psalm 18:26). Then as God shows Himself pure to us, we show ourselves pure to others. *The purer we become, the more we're able to see the purity of God and follow His example more accurately.*

One way we follow His example is by living a life of unselfishness. God's Word describes the maturing Christian's growth: "Now that you have purified yourselves by obeying the truth so that you have sincere love for your brothers, *love one another deeply*, from the heart.... Therefore, rid yourselves of all malice and all deceit, hypocrisy, envy, and slander of every kind...so that...you may *grow up in your salvation*, now that you have tasted that the Lord is good" (1 Peter 1:22; 2:1–3, italics added). Once you've rid yourself of sin (by confession), tasted His goodness (by salvation), love Him sincerely

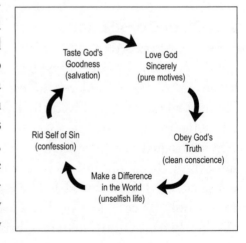

Taste God's Goodness (salvation)

Love God Sincerely (pure motives)

Obey God's Truth (clean conscience)

Make a Difference in the World (unselfish life)

Rid Self of Sin (confession)

(out of pure motives), and obey (with a clean conscience), then you are able to make a difference in the world (through an unselfish life).

4. Clean Thoughts and Language

Perhaps you've noticed that people who become Christians suddenly begin to clean up their language. When Jesus indwells your heart, a certain awe for God fills your whole being. Speaking without profanity or off-color slang is one way you live out deep heart purity in your interactions with others. Jesus remarked that your words reflect what's in your heart. In Matthew 15, He says, "What comes out of [a man's] mouth, that is what makes him 'unclean'" (v. 11) and, further, "the things that come out of the mouth come from the heart" (v. 18). Even when profanity is a persistent problem from Christians' past, they manage to purify their language as they mature by working on their hearts and minds. Paul said, "Whatever is true, whatever is noble, whatever is right, whatever is *pure*, whatever is lovely, whatever is admirable—if anything is excellent or praiseworthy—think about such things (Philippians 4:8, italics added). Sometimes God washes new Christians' thoughts and mouths clean instantly. In most cases, however, it takes years of dedication and sanctification (as God sanctifies, or purifies them). He says, "Then will I purify the lips of the peoples [translated from the Hebrew "in pure language"], that all of them may call on the name of the LORD" (Zephaniah 3:9). One of the marks of maturing Christians with pure hearts is their clean language.

List the main precepts from # 4:

Then pray the following verse from Psalms:

May the words of my mouth and the meditation of my heart be pleasing in your sight, O LORD, my Rock and my Redeemer. (Psalm 19:14)

5. Giving Without Expecting Anything in Return

Growing in unselfishness toward others, you'll not only begin to concentrate on clean thoughts and language, but also you'll recognize unselfishness in other areas of your physical life. Last week one of my church's Bible study teachers, Joe Cox, told this story: A gardener in England saved a wealthy family's drowning child. As a reward, the father asked if the gardener wanted anything in return. Though surprised, he didn't have to think long: he asked for the family to pay for his son Alexander's education. The grateful family provided the education, and the son, Alexander Fleming, grew up to develop penicillin. Years later, the saved son of the benefactor family, Winston Churchill, was deathly ill with a raging infection. Alexander's antibiotic saved Winston's life (which the Fleming family had then saved twice)! Twentieth-century citizens often asked, "Where would the world be without Winston Churchill?" Many also asked, "Where would the world be without Alexander Fleming?"—and without his father, who sacrificed, doing the noble thing, without expecting anything further in return.

If you want to mature spiritually, then out of a grateful, pure heart, you will deny yourself, take up the cross of self-sacrifice, and follow Christ (Matthew 16:24).

6. A God-Centered Focus, Not a World-Centered Focus

As you mature, your lifestyle will change from a more world-centered approach to a God-centered approach. Paul saw Ephesus, a Greek city of pagan gods and worldly pleasure, as a fertile evangelistic field where people really needed a God-centered focus. He advised Timothy:

> *Stay there in Ephesus so that you may command certain men not to teach false doctrines any longer trusting in pagan principles, not Christ based] nor to devote themselves to myths [depending on traditions to save] and endless genealogies [relying on royal, commendable birth to justify them before God]. These promote controversies rather than God's work—which is by faith. The goal of this command is love, which comes from a pure heart and a good conscience and a sincere faith. Some have wandered away from these and turned to meaningless talk [complex oration or trivial jokes]. (1 Timothy 1:3–6)*

Paul could have spoken these words yesterday. As a maturing Christian, instead of falling for the postmodern world's philosophy, fill your day with praise of the true God: "My mouth is filled with your praise, declaring your splendor all day long" (Psalm 71:8).

7. A Need for Refining the Heart and Life

Though all Christians do sin from time to time, our hearts can remain pure. As you drift away from Christ, you recognize your need for purification, turn to God, align your will with His, and allow Him to sanctify you through the purifying process, anew every day. "He will be like a refiner's fire…and refine them like gold and silver" (Malachi 3:2–3). The closer you stay to His heart, the less sin you commit, and the purer your heart becomes.

Refiner's Fire

In the 1990s, our state denominational staff in California labored for months preparing a training conference at Hume Lake, a conference center nestled in the snow-capped Sierra Mountains around an azure-blue lake. Our staff prepared programs for general sessions; arranged for musicians, dramatists, and speakers in worship services and small workshops; checked rooming lists; stocked a book store; and planned meals, recreation, and study experiences. Then a guest speaker told the church staffs there: "All the planning and scurrying to get this extravaganza ready may have been done just to refine one lonely pastor's heart. Make no mistake about it: God has orchestrated all the preparation and planning. No one else. He has a purpose for *you* at this very place. He wants to refine your heart." Those mature Christians, mostly pastors and church leaders, knew they had a need to be refined. Year by year mature Christians keep close to the Refiner, willing to go through the fire to find a pure heart. God says, "I will thoroughly purge away your dross and remove all your impurities" (Isaiah 1:25).

How do you see manifestations of each of these seven characteristics of a pure heart in your own life?

1.

2.

3.

4.

5.

6.

7.

Discuss with a study partner.

Decide in which areas you are in need of more maturity:

Today's surgeons perform miracles on the human heart, but nothing is more of a miracle than the heart surgery that takes place when you ask Jesus to indwell your heart. It is *spiritual heart surgery.* He promises, "I will give you a new heart and put a new spirit in you; I will remove from you your heart of stone and give you a heart of flesh.... You will be my people" (Ezekiel 36:26, 28). The way you open your heart for Christ's open-heart surgery determines how much your heart can change and at which times it changes. God is always there, ready and able to change you. Your part is cleaning out the junk to make more room for Him. There may have been no room in the inn for the Savior on the night He was born, but there's ample room in your heart. A maturing Christian is constantly on guard, aware of the surgery going on, kicking out evil from time to time, and welcoming the purifying heart changes.

Above all else, guard your heart, for it is the well-spring of life! (Proverbs 4:23)

M&M: *Ministry and Missions Moment*
D. A. Ousley devotes a chapter of his book *The Way of Holiness* to driving. (Does that seem to be a strange topic to include in a book about spiritual maturity?) He says *the way you drive is an indication*

of your spiritual maturity. If you don't drive with courtesy, patience, and unselfishness, then you are not a truly mature Christian.

Match your driving record to the seven characteristics of a pure heart in this study. Do you drive with pure motives, unselfish actions, and a clear conscience? Do you have good thoughts and language (and gestures)? Do you give the right of way, without expecting anything in return? Is your driving God centered? Does it need refining? Pray with your eyes and pure heart open as you drive this week, and perform a ministry checkup on your driving.

Deeper Still: *Mystery Revealed*

Meditate on this mysterious principle this week: *Purity of heart is not only a spiritual characteristic, but is also a physical one.* As you allow God to purify your heart, your body also becomes purified. The writer of Hebrews said, "Let us draw near to God with a *sincere heart*, having our hearts sprinkled to cleanse us from a guilty conscience and having our bodies washed with *pure* water" (Hebrews 10:22, italics added). Pray for purity in both areas.

—— Study 4 ——

Godly Wisdom

The world offers abundant examples of incredible stupidity. A popular newspaper article told the story of "Jerry," an out-of-work man who lived near LAX, the Los Angeles airport. Each day he spent long hours watching planes come and go. One day he purchased a large weather balloon, anchored his lawn chair to the ground with several tethers, filled the balloon with helium, tied it to the chair, sat in his chair with a hatchet, cut the tether ropes, and shot upward. Jerry smiled; his plan had been successful.

However, his plan was not exact. When he drifted out over the Pacific and reached 11,000 feet, planes radioed the LAX tower. A Coast Guard helicopter rescued him; then he was arrested for being in the path of oncoming air traffic. One of the rescuers asked why he did it. His answer: "I wondered what flying was like, so I thought I'd try it."

We have good examples of absurdity, such as adventurers who go over Niagara Falls in a barrel, thieves in convenience stores who try to escape with their stolen goods by pushing against an unlocked door marked "Pull," or a bank robber who succeeds in the robbery, but accidentally leaves a check at the teller's window with his name and address.

Even those whom the world admires because of their great discoveries sometimes appear to lack wisdom. Descartes got inside a wood stove, emerged covered with soot, and said profoundly, "I think; therefore I am." Jean-Paul Sartre said life is absurd. I believe most non-Christian philosophers also believe they are brilliant thinkers.

On the other hand, *Christian* philosophers already know their limitations in God's world. They begin with the following premises:

🐦 God is all knowing; we are not.

🐦 He is good; we are sinful.

🐦 Because of the Fall, our character is flawed; His is not.

🐦 Our earthly wisdom is insufficient; His wisdom is abundant and sufficient.

🐦 We need to depend on Him for all spiritual wisdom.

🐦 At best, we have a scattered, greedy mind-set, sometimes distracted by possessions, gadgets, improper motives, and negative feelings. He exhibits a complete mind-set, focused on our developing a spiritual life of holy communion.

The Mind of God and What It Means

So how do you get this focus, this holy mind-set? You obtain it from Christ. Paul says in 1 Corinthians 2:16, "We have the mind of Christ." Shrugging, people ask, "How can *we* understand His mind?" Isaiah asked the same question hundreds of years ago: "Who has understood the mind of the LORD?" (Isaiah 40:13). The answer is found in Romans 8:27: "He *who searches our hearts* knows the mind of the Spirit, because the Spirit intercedes for the saints in accordance with God's will" (italics added). Who is the One *who searches our hearts*? Jesus, our mediator for understanding the mind of our Father, through His Holy Spirit. Scholars agree that these words of Isaiah point to Christ as "a shoot…from the stump of Jesse" (King David's father, from whose lineage Jesus was born into the household of Mary and Joseph): "The Spirit of the LORD will rest on him—the Spirit of wisdom and of understanding, the Spirit of counsel and of power, the Spirit of knowledge and of the fear of the LORD—and he will delight in the fear of the LORD" (Isaiah 11:1–3). Look at these characteristics of the mind of Christ: *wisdom, understanding, counsel, power, knowledge, and fear of the Lord.*

Jesus says, "I am in the Father and the Father is in me.… I will ask the Father, and he will give you another Counselor to be with you forever—the Spirit of truth.… You know him, for he lives with you and will be in you" (John 14:11, 16–17). Look back at Paul's words in 1 Corinthians 2:16. Who are the *we* in that verse? Paul is speaking of all Christians, not just of himself or the other apostles. If it is true that *we—all Christians*—can have the mind of Christ, then how do we obtain it? Jesus said, "Everything that I learned from my Father I have made known to you.… The Father will give you whatever you ask in my name" (John 15:15–16). Christians seeking the *mind* of Christ should start by seeking Christ Himself.

Do you know for sure you are a Christian? Do you know absolutely that you will go to heaven when you die? If not, there is a way to be sure. Read John 20:31 and 1 John 5:13. God has provided His Word, the Bible, so that you can know for sure that you have eternal life. Take these simple steps:

1. Think of sins you've committed (bad things you've done) against God or others.
2. Ask Him to forgive you from those sins.
3. Ask Jesus to come into your heart to help you live for Him daily.
4. Praise God that you can go to heaven since Jesus died for your sins.
5. Promise to begin a relationship with Him: reading your Bible, praying, and joining a fellowship of other Christians where you can learn more about Him.

What are your thoughts about accepting Christ as your Savior?

Share with your pastor, a Christian friend, or a study partner.

The Wisdom of Christ

Once you know absolutely that you are a Christian, then you begin the process of obtaining the mind of Christ. Start by asking for His wisdom. "The fear of the LORD is the beginning of wisdom" (Proverbs 9:10). Jerome defined *insight* as "only mortal knowledge," but he defined *wisdom* as "knowledge of divine and human proportions." Human knowledge is visible, he said, but divine knowledge is invisible. Christ had wisdom in His relationships, in His prayer life, and in His ministry. He kept a balance in His earthly life by showing love to those in need, fellowshipping with friends and family, and drawing away from crowds for times of prayer and renewal. He didn't make wise choices, ushering serenity and order into His life, by making a to-do list, a vision statement, or a five-year plan. Jesus knew how to make wise choices because He was connected to the Truth of God Almighty! He could be wise because He had eternal wisdom. And so can you.

The Counsel of Christ

One of the most exciting thoughts of the mature Christian is the idea of maintaining a relationship with God Himself! Once you accept Christ and begin growing in wisdom, you'll find the counsel of Christ a mainstay. He is the "Wonderful Counselor; Mighty God" (Isaiah 9:6). The personal relationship with God through the Holy Spirit is an incredible blessing that no other religion on earth offers! We build a trust, solid foundation for family and community life, and a bulwark against adversity. No matter how hard life is— if I lose all family, friends, every familiarity in life—I know who my Comforter, the Rock of Ages, is: the Wonderful Counselor, Prince of Peace. When you have *no peace or rest*, you can count on Him!

What kind of pain, loss, or disaster is now facing you?

Do you think God cares about your troubles? Why or why not?

Read the following Scriptures and list ways God speaks through these words:

Psalm 9:9

Psalm 46:1

John 14:1–4, 27

2 Timothy 1:7

The Knowledge of Christ

Through intimate relationship, the Spirit also gives us other things; He teaches us as He counsels. Jesus said, "The Counselor, the Holy Spirit, whom the Father will send in my name, will teach you all things and will remind you of everything I have said to you" (John 14:26). As we've seen earlier, His Spirit gives us knowledge as an internal voice, from the mind of God to the mind of a woman or a man: "This is the covenant I will make with them after that time, says the Lord. I will put my laws in their hearts, and I will write them on their minds" (Hebrews 10:16). God says, "Be transformed by the renewing of your mind. Then you will be able to test and approve what God's will is—his good, pleasing and perfect will" (Romans 12:2). To have knowledge of the will of God…just think of it! And it's yours as you love God, listen to Him, and obey His precepts. There's no doubt about it: as you grow closer to Christ, you'll be renewed in mind, body, soul, and spirit!

The Power of Christ

Here's the most exciting part of growing in Christ: you'll find a reserve of power within you that you hardly knew you had. Christians can speak up, write dynamically, teach the Word, focus on Bible study for hours, minister to people who need help, and counsel others in a *mystical* way. You will often hear a Christian say, "I don't know exactly what I said, but she said she heard God speaking through me." As you listen to Him, you're empowered by the Sovereign God to do amazing things! Jesus said, "I tell you the truth, anyone who has faith in me will do what I have been doing. He will do even greater things than these, because I am going to the Father" (John 14:12).

We have Jesus, who was one of us and knew the limitations of being human, now living in heaven to be our advocate with our Heavenly Father! As a result, we can do unbelievable things: "When we are cursed, we bless; when we are persecuted, we endure it; when we are slandered, we answer kindly" (1 Corinthians 4:12–13). Mature Christians face trials and temptations triumphantly, calmly—even meeting death with courage.

The Fear of God

I was present in a meeting of executives who questioned Dr. Dellanna O'Brien about decisions she had made. One of them asked if she were not afraid of repercussions from her decisions. She answered, "Sir, I am afraid of no one except God Himself." That strong statement is the mark of a mature Christian. Through the centuries, martyrs have died by stoning, hanging, shooting, torture, and burning at the stake—unafraid, because they had the fear of no one on earth, nothing alive or dead, except their Sovereign God.

For comforting Scriptures about God, read the following and write in your own words what each of these means in your life:

Psalm 27:1

Psalm 56:3

Proverbs 3:24

Jeremiah 1:8

Matthew 8:26; 10:28–31

Mark 5:36

Hebrews 13:6

The Delight of Knowing God's Mind

Although mature Christians fear, or have awesome reverence for God, they're not terrified by His presence. God said, "Do not be afraid, for I am with you" many times (Genesis 26:24; Isaiah 41:10; 43:5; Luke 1:30). Remember the final words of Isaiah 11:1–3: "He will delight in the fear of the LORD." One distinguishing mark of mature Christians is that they can laugh in the face of danger and keep a sense of humor through tribulation (1 Peter 1:6–8). Memorize these words from a mature Christian: *My happiness does not depend on outer circumstances; I have deep-down joy from God Himself that fills me every day.* If worried or anxious, repeat this assurance, to be "made new in the attitude of your mind," as suggested in Ephesians 4:23. Paul said, "God hath not given us the

spirit of fear; but of power, and of love, and of a sound mind"
(2 Timothy 1:7 KJV). Even Christians who've had treatment for
deep depression can look toward the light of Christ and joke about
circumstances. They don't live by the whims of other people or
each day's events, but are "of sound mind" (literally, [Gr.] "self-
disciplined") and optimistic. Taking delight in knowing God's
mind can heal a multitude of ills. That delight can also lead to harmony with other Christians. If you experience friction with any
other Christian, pray according to the following exercise.

Read Matthew 5:21–24, 38–47. Then complete these sentences:

I have no delight in other Christians when...

**I've had at least one argument with another Christian that has
not been resolved because...**

**In the Sermon on the Mount, Jesus said this about being angry
with a brother...**

If someone strikes me on the cheek, I should...

If I have an enemy, I should...

I will reclaim the delight I have in God, resolving to walk in harmony with other Christians in these ways:

Peter's first epistle calls this delight of mind "lively hope" (1:3 KJV)—that brings delight and cheer. He also says, "Gird up the loins of your mind, be sober, and hope to the end for the grace that is to be brought unto you at the revelation of Jesus Christ" (1:13 KJV). A *living hope* verifies we've been born again and assures we have *cause* for delight. Oswald Chambers said, "Keep a sense of humour in divine things as well as in human things." Mature Christians know they don't have to be somber to be spiritually mature. You can rejoice *in* God, *with* God, and *for* God!

Read each of the following Scriptures twice. Then write what you discovered the second time that you did not notice the first time you read.

1 Corinthians 1:10

Philippians 2:3

Philippians 4:2

1 Peter 3:8 and 4:1

2 Thessalonians 2:2

Revelation 17:13

Say several times today and in the days that follow: "This is the day the LORD has made; I will rejoice and be glad in it" (Psalm 118:24, personalized). After a few days, come back to this spot and write how your life has changed by repeating this verse.

M&M: *Ministry and Missions Moment*

God has focused His mind on *you*. His Word says, "The LORD hath been mindful of us: he will bless us" (Psalm 115:12 KJV). Be mindful always of His covenant (1 Chronicles 16:15). Brother Lawrence tells in *The Practice of the Presence of God* that he experienced a oneness with the mind of Christ as he prayed while cleaning stables. The quiet of the stables provided a time to focus on Christ. What can you do to help others focus their minds on Him? How about providing quiet moments for preschoolers' parents? Or teach teenagers to withdraw from their friends—and the music plugged into their ears—for a time to listen to God, absorbing His mind. Decide one way you'll provide a time to share the mind of Christ.

Deeper Still: *Mystery Revealed*

God says, "Come now, let us reason together" (Isaiah 1:18). Set aside a time daily for reasoning with God. Bring a pen and journal to a quiet place. Listen to God's logic and write the thoughts He brings to mind. Here are my favorite logical verses about knowledge, but you may choose your own: Isaiah 26:3; 46:8–10; Romans 1:28; 2 Corinthians 3:12–14; Philippians 3:15–16; and James 1:2–8;. *Meditate on the mysteries God reveals as you grow quiet before Him.*

Study 5

Outrageous Prayers

In Anaheim, California, around the corner from Disneyland, sits a church with a hundred members. Thousands of tourists visit the theme park each year. "Roger," the pastor, told me how his church began to witness to them: members bought yearly tickets to Disneyland. Each Saturday they met international tourists standing in line at the gate. They spent the day together, enjoying rides and eating together in the restaurants. As the day progressed, the Christians shared the plan of salvation with new friends from around the world. Many people accepted Christ as their Savior; the church followed up by connecting them with missionaries overseas.

New Filipino friends came often to Disneyland; as a result, Californians went to the Philippines on several missions trips. Leaving for America, Roger once asked, "What do you need?"

The answer came, "Ten thousand tons of wheat." Roger's heart sank. He reminded them that Anaheim is urban, but told them that his church would pray about what to do, trusting God, who possessed tons of wheat. When they got home, Roger displayed a map of the US and asked members to pray whether the place with wheat was east or west of the Mississippi River. He says, "We prayed until we reached consensus. It was east of the Mississippi river." Then they folded the map in half again. Was it in the northern or southern half of the eastern US? A week later, they had their answer. It was in the northern half.

Using this method, they continued to fold the map until they came to consensus that the wheat was in Illinois. Folding a state map, they prayed again: east, west, north, or south? They narrowed their focus to two counties, then one city. Ordering a city phone book, they narrowed by prayer as they had in the past: names in front or back of the alphabet? in which column? Finally, the church stalled in their prayers, after narrowing to two names.

"We'll call both," Roger said. He dialed one, and a man answered. "When I asked him if he had tons of wheat, he laughed, saying, "No, I have no wheat, but if you find anybody with free wheat, I'll ship it to Los Angeles for you. I own a shipping company." Roger dialed the second number; a man answered. Roger says, "When I gave him my request, he was silent for a moment. Then he said, 'I was wondering what to do with this 10,000-ton excess from last year's crop. My new crop's ready to be stored in the silos holding last year's excess. You can have last year's wheat.'"

Roger grinned. "One week ago we shipped ten thousand tons of wheat to Filipinos who needed it desperately."

To an outrageous prayer, God gave an outrageous answer!

Don't be afraid to pray courageously and outrageously. Mature Christians trust God so much that they pray outrageous prayers—no matter what others think. God says, "Do not be anxious about anything, but in everything, by prayer and petition, with thanksgiving, present your requests to God" (Philippians 4:6). Notice one word: *everything*—no matter how big or how small.

Prayer Practice

Outrageous pray-ers usually don't start praying powerfully at the beginning of their Christian experience. They grow in maturity the way a child's body grows: through the maturation process, one step at a time. Many experts give advice on praying, but the supreme rule to remember is this: to become a mature pray-er, you will grow deeper and deeper still in God's Spirit as your fleshly *self* becomes less and less during prayer. At my age, I can see Christians of all ages growing deeper in Christ in six levels. I call them the *six deeper-still levels:*

Six Deeper-Still Levels

❦ Level 1: Surface Prayer

This, of course, is the most shallow level of praying, which has several practical examples:

Praying Words: Most mature Christians have heard someone praying words, reading out of a prayer book, or repeating a memorized prayer. This can be real praying, of course, but it can also be insincere praying, since the pray-er is mouthing words.

Practicing Model Prayers: Prayer power is developed over the weeks, months, and years of your life. I began as did many children: "Now I lay me down to sleep, I pray the Lord my soul to keep." I practiced that model prayer nightly until I became a preteen. An immature Christian may begin by reading Jesus's example, known as the Lord's Prayer: "Our Father which art in heaven…" (Matthew 6:9–13 KJV). You may also follow a scriptural prayer of David, Paul, John, or Peter.

Professional Prayers: Sometimes mature Christians engage in a type of leadership that can contain a false prayer without any feeling or the Holy Spirit's leadership. You might say, "Function follows form"; that is, the form is uppermost in the pray-er's mind, who suspends an important function of prayer (fellowship with God through the Holy Spirit) so the leader can lead or instruct others in prayer.

☙ Level 2: Selfish Prayer

The day after I became a Christian, my parents took me shopping on our town's main street. As they shopped at a vegetable stand, I watched a boy with an ice cream cone. His dark skin shone as the vanilla ice cream glistened on his lips and cheeks.

I saw a sign over the drug store door saying ice cream was on sale for five cents.

As the sun beat down on that July day, I thought, *I'd like ice cream to cool off.... I'm a Christian now; I'll pray with power and God will answer.* I bowed my head and closed my eyes, with people passing. "Lord," I said, "I want a nickel for an ice cream cone. A nickel, a nickel...five cents, five cents...." When I opened my eyes, to my surprise, a nickel lay between my toes. Had it been there all along? Did a kind passerby place it there while my eyes were closed? I only know that God answered my prayer instantly!

I've often wondered why God answered such a selfish prayer from a little girl. I believe it was to teach me the power of prayer. From that miraculous moment, I've been convinced God answers prayer in dynamic ways. As a maturing Christian, you also remember your weak attempts at prayer that began selfishly.

Stop now and thank God for His maturing you in prayer.

Think of your early attempts at prayer. Write your memories:

Praise God for the way He has nudged you along in your prayer maturity. List signs of maturity in prayer:

Ask for faith to pray more courageous and outrageous prayers.

Sometimes you may focus on perceived needs that exist in your selfish heart, not in your renewed mind. Perhaps you have a need: a new car, money in the bank, a boyfriend or girlfriend, a child, a good job...the list continues. However, although you, as a mature Christian, do pray for your needs to be met, those needs are not the primary focus of prayer. As a Christian matures, he or she begins to move from the selfish to the unselfish scale of maturity. On the Road to Maturity Chart, place an X where you are in your prayer development. Place a star (★) where you'd like to be.

Road to Maturity

Selfish Prayer – – – – – – Unselfish Prayer

❧ Level 3: Serious Prayer

A simple definition of *serious prayer* is "a prayer you pray when you get serious about praying." Most Christians cling to God when they're in trouble: financial stress, family problems, loss of job, bereavement, or fear. Early talk-show host Jack Parr said he recognized God was real when, in a small boat near a beachhead, the toughest man in the army suddenly fell on his knees, praying before facing the enemy. When the chips are down and things get serious, you depend on God. My father brought home a saying from World War II: "There are no atheists in foxholes." God created us to worship Him, and we automatically grow toward Him in time of trouble. "God is our refuge and strength, a very present help in trouble" (Psalm 46:1 KJV).

Once when I needed prayer, I sought advice from a friend, who told me, "Seek God and **PUSH: P**ray **U**ntil **S**omething **H**appens." When you face serious times, remember, "Present your requests to God" (Philippians 4:6). "And all things, whatever you ask in prayer, believing, you shall receive" (Matthew 21:22 NKJV).

Times of serious prayer lead to Christian maturity because you learn more in hard times than in easy times. Comfort causes most humans to become lazy and fail to seek God's deeper truths. Jennifer Kennedy Dean, author of several books on prayer, says Christians need to "discover the difference between a prayer life [an activity] and a praying life [a life]." You will find the praying life opening up during times of serious prayer, and the "life-absorbing relationship with God" becomes your entire life. (For Jennifer Kennedy Dean's prayer materials contact www.prayinglife.org or newhopepublishers.com.)

❧ Level 4: Self-Reconnection Prayer

Even though our needs may be met—even in serious times—most of us fall into deeper trouble from time to time: sin attacks us; we revert to our "old, carnal" nature and lash out at others; we harbor anger; or we succumb to lust, greed, and other depravities. When these sins occur, our prayer life suffers because we have lost relationship with God.

David strayed from God in the worst way. In moments of comfort and plenty, his careless boredom led to lust; lust led to sexual immorality with Bathsheba; sexual immorality led to the murder of Bathsheba's husband, Uriah; and murder led to dire consequences. David desperately needed to be reconnected to his power source. He later prayed, "O LORD, have mercy on me; heal me, for I have sinned against you" (Psalm 41:4). Scripture says, "If I had cherished sin in my heart, the LORD would not have listened" (Psalm 66:18).

On the contrary, Jesus said the key to Christian life is a connection to Him: "I am the vine; you are the branches. If a man remains in me and I in him, he will bear much fruit; *apart from me you can do nothing.* If anyone does not remain in me, he is like a branch that is thrown away and withers; such branches are picked up, thrown into the fire and burned" (John 15:5–6, italics added). Does being apart from the True Vine mean you are worthless? Hardly. God loves you with an everlasting love. David says, "In my integrity you uphold me and set me in your presence forever. Praise be to the LORD" (Psalm 41:12–13).

David, unfortunately, like many of us, was an off-and-on believer. God loved him, forgiving him many times, but he suffered for his times of disconnection. Like David, Paul said, "It is no longer I myself who do it, but it is sin living in me.... I have the desire to do what is good, but I cannot carry it out. For what I do is not the good I want to do; no, the evil I do not want to do—this I keep on doing" (Romans 7:17–19). As we mature as Christians, we become less tentative and more steady in our connections to our power source. Jesus said, "If you remain in me and my words remain in you, ask whatever you wish, and it will be given you. This is to my Father's glory" (John 15:7–8). Maturing Christians are well aware that *success teaches nothing* and that it is only in surrendering, yielding, and reconnecting that prayer changes us and satisfies God.

❧ Level 5: Constant Prayer

Nothing is more exciting than keeping in touch with Jesus all day. Yesterday I drove across three states, praying in the car with open eyes, which I'd learned to do with my husband years ago. He had an old blue pickup he called his prayermobile, in which he prayed often. When we had hard decisions to make, we drove around in the prayermobile, praying aloud until we received an answer. As you mature as a Christian, you'll find yourself praying constantly. You pray with your eyes open as you walk, drive, or shop. Most maturing Christians can tell you they've had similar experiences with praying all day long. They come into the presence of God as a matter of habit—a deepening habit—that continues through the hours like a visit with a good friend.

Paul wrote: "Be joyful always; pray continually; give thanks in all circumstances, for this is God's will for you in Christ Jesus" (1 Thessalonians 5:16–18). Some mature Christians have noticed that God's Word says, "pray continually," that is, intermittently; not "pray continuously," that is, without taking a breath or doing any other tasks, such as ministry or missions endeavors, allowing for Christian service. Maturing Christians are busy about their Father's business, yet remain in an attitude of prayer.

❧ Level 6: Surrendered Prayer

As you mature, you'll undergo a change that exudes confidence: No matter whether God answers with an instant "Yes!"; replies slowly, "No, My child"; or mysteriously has you wait in silence for years, you recognize that prayer is a matter of communication with the

Father, not a place to register complaints, get instant answers, or beg for selfish wants. Your humble soul surrenders to His. A prayer practitioner is willing to do outrageous things as God's Word and His Spirit lead. As a maturing Christian, you weigh the cost of your prayers and then step out in faith.

God says, "Go, stand and speak in the temple to the people all the words of this life" (Acts 5:20 KJV). Mature Christians share what they know about prayer and pray unselfish prayers for others: intercession for friends who are hurting physically, socially, financially, or spiritually. They pray for extended family and church family. They stand in the gap for hurting pastors, church staff, Bible study teachers, and deacons. They dare hold up political issues and injustices before God, asking Him for breakthroughs of the gospel all around the world. "Let his kingdom reach from sea to sea" (see Psalm 72:8). They pray "Thy will be done," even when they know God's will is not their will.

Ancient classifications tell us much about Old Testament prayers: the psalmist used these conventions as he prayed, just as you do today: *Tephillah*, supplication; *tehillah*, praise; *lehazkir*, petition; *letodah*, giving thanks; and *mizmor*, hymn, or prayer singing. As prayer warriors practice sincerely, they may use Scripture portions for more prayer power.

However, in learning to pray, we don't always start off praying with power. The figure on the next page shows six stages of prayers. As a pray-er, you may begin with surface prayer (stage 1), just saying or mouthing words, and remain in the shallows as evil seems far away. Then as you face sin and temptation, you begin selfish prayer (stage 2) for your own well-being. Succumbing to temptation leads to guilt, stress, and serious prayer (stage 3). As you begin to recognize sin and realize your unworthiness, you take a deeper step toward God. Evil continues to attack, and you continue to fall short of the life you yearn for. As you grow closer to God, you pray

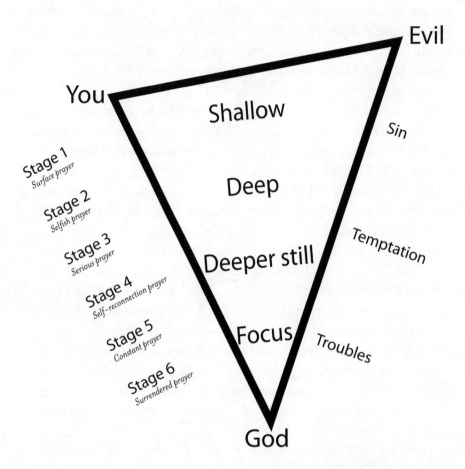

self-reconnection prayer (stage 4), asking humbly for forgiveness. Evil encroaches on you, coming closer moment by moment as you, a maturing Christian, come closer to God to reconnect with Him. As you grow deeper still in your understanding of Him and the power of evil, you remain in constant prayer (stage 5). Growing deeper still in wisdom and godliness as you desperately face troubles caused by evil, you perceive spiritual light and see eternal truth. Your focus narrows; you look only at the face of God as you surrender in prayer. In spite of troubles and distractions, your faith goes to the ultimate depths, closer and ever closer to Him in surrendered prayer (stage 6). The closer you come to the heart of God, the more painfully aware you are of your own shortcomings. With ever-deeper humility, your faith in God's answers is steeled; your will is bent into His. At your deepest point, your heart and will are one with God's.

In November 1989 when the Brandenburg Gate fell in Berlin, beginning the end of the Cold War, I watched the incredible event on television. I went to a prayer group meeting the next day, and expressed my disbelief that The Wall—which had stood for decades as an atheistic symbol of godless authority—was dismantled without bloodshed! A wonderful prayer warrior, Nell Haggert, said quietly, "I'm not surprised; I've been praying for that for ten years." I was stunned. I had never prayed for the wall to come down. I began to think of my prayer power in a different way.

Years later I read the story behind the headlines: weeks before the wall came down, a small group of Berlin Christians met in a home to pray. The group grew, finally becoming too big for the home. Thousands prayed in halls, as the number continued to grow nightly. One Monday night they spilled over into the streets, numbering more than five million! Peacefully and quietly praying, they walked slowly to the Brandenburg Gate and took down the wall. As they prayed, they became His hands and feet, climbing up, taking one chunk at a time, until the wall was down! You become an instrument of God's peace as you pray, allowing Him to lead you in changing the world, one brick at a time.

M&M: *Ministry and Missions Moment*

I heard these words on the radio this week: "If you have Jesus on your lips, you should have the cross on your back." *The prayer of a mature Christian explodes exponentially in his physical life. You live out a life of sacrifice as you dare to pray outrageous prayers.*

Francis of Assisi prayed, "Lord, make me be an instrument of thy peace. Where there is hatred, let me sow love; where there is injury, pardon; where there is doubt, faith; where there is despair, hope; where there is darkness, light; where there is sadness, joy. O, Divine Master, grant that we may seek not so much to be consoled as to console; to be understood as to understand; to be loved as to love. For it is in giving that we receive; it is in pardoning that we are pardoned; and it is in dying that we are born to eternal life." Put feet on your prayers, mature Christian.

Deeper Still: *Mystery Revealed*

Prayer is always mysterious. It crosses all barriers of time, place, mortality, and dimension. Prayer changes many things, but the most important thing it changes is *you*. As you sacrifice self, as you intercede, your heart and mind mature through prayer. *From adversity springs outrageous prayer.*

Unit 2

———————— • ————————

CHARACTERISTICS OF MATURE LIVING

Oh, I am nothing, Lord; I worship at Your feet.
Please help me be Your servant in ever-humbler ways.

Almighty, send me out, out, out—with wide, courageous faith.
The ground may fall beneath my feet; my earthly body failing;

But Solid God, my Rock, I cling to You, depending....
Mighty palpable majesty, bring order and simplicity.

Be still my soul, O give me rest, and take me deeper still,
Till I am bent to be just like the heart and face of God.

Study 6

A Servant Heart

One afternoon a man hit his finger with a hammer. It hurt so much he had to stop his project. That night, each part of his body sympathized. The other fingers shot out sympathy pains for their fellow finger. The arm ached in sympathy. The legs were restless to show they cared. The eyes stayed open all night, on alert to help if needed. The heart raced, sympathetic with each throb. The stomach rumbled; the knees doubled up in pain. Each part of the body served the part that hurt. The man didn't appreciate his body working to support the hurt finger, but saw in his own body an example of the coordination of the Church, the body of Christ. The church body was designed to serve and support the other parts. God says, "Speaking the truth in love, we will in all things grow up into him who is the Head, that is, Christ. From him the whole body, joined and held together by every supporting ligament, grows and builds itself up in love, as each part does its work" (Ephesians 4:15–16). As growing, maturing Christians, we want to be servants, supporting ligaments for the rest of the body of Christ.

The Bible is full of servant examples. King David, perhaps the greatest Israeli king, often called himself "servant of the Lord, my God." From the time he was a simple shepherd till the time he ruled over all 12 tribes of Israel, he had a servant's heart. He chose his younger son, Solomon, over murderous son Adonijah, who haughtily had tried to assume the kingship (1 Kings 1:5–10) because Solomon also was known as a servant (1 Kings 1:26), following even the hard commands of the Master (1 Kings 2:26–46).

Give Your Servant a Discerning Heart

One night God appeared to King Solomon in a dream: "And God said, 'Ask for whatever you want me to give you.' Solomon answered, 'You have shown great kindness to your servant, my father David, because he was faithful to you and righteous and upright in heart. Now, O LORD my God, you have made your servant [Solomon] king.... So give your servant a discerning heart to govern your people and to distinguish between right and wrong'" (1 Kings 3:5–7, 9). When Solomon dedicated the beautiful temple to God (1 Kings 8:62–66), the people of the kingdom were "glad in heart" for all the good things the two servant kings had done.

Jesus is our example of the servant heart: He took on the form of a *servant* (Philippians 2:7), teaching His disciples to be servants daily. Later the disciple John said he heard an angel, who spoke to "his *servant* John" (Revelation 1:1). In the first century A.D., the apostle Paul wrote of servanthood in his advice to the early churches, using the word *Dulas* [Gr.], "slave," or "employee." He says, "Guard your work so people won't think bad of Christ" (see Ephesians 6:5–8). He also said to another group of Christians, "I have made myself a *servant* of all" (see 1 Corinthians 9:19). It's clear the early Church thought of themselves as servants.

God loves a servant heart, keeping us near His heart: "I live in a high and holy place, but also with him who is contrite and lowly in spirit, to revive the spirit of the lowly, and to revive the heart of the contrite" (Isaiah 57:15). A friend told me when I was sad, "God has everything in the world, and He can boss you around." Yet she and I agreed that we serve God because we're *freed*, not *forced* to serve. We love Him; we choose to be His slaves. "O LORD, truly I am your servant.... You have freed me from my chains" (Psalm 116:16). Can you echo this prayer of a servant?

Based on Psalm 116:16, how has God freed you from your chains?

List below what kinds of things place people in bondage:

Identify a few of the things you listed that *you* have experienced personally and from which God has freed you:

Praise God now that He has freed you from your chains.

Actions of a Servant

God says, "His servants will serve him" (Revelation 22:3), but here are other specific actions of servants:

- ❦ **A servant depends on God's promises.** "Your promises have been thoroughly tested, and your servant loves them" (Psalm 119:140).
- ❦ **A servant meditates.** "Your servant will meditate on your decrees" (Psalm 119:23).
- ❦ **A servant reads Scripture.** "I have hidden your word in my heart that I might not sin against you" (Psalm 119:11).
- ❦ **A servant seeks the face of God.** "Make your face shine upon your servant" (Psalm 119:135).
- ❦ **A servant earns God's delight.** "A king delights in a wise servant" (Proverbs 14:35).
- ❦ **A servant is focused on one master.** "No servant can serve two masters" (Luke 16:13).

Besides describing these actions of a Christian servant, God's Word gives a warning: "Who is blind like the one committed to me, blind like the servant of the LORD? *You have seen many things, but have paid no attention*" (Isaiah 42:19–20). The first time I read these words, I was surprised. I couldn't believe God would say such a thing to me, yet that morning, He was speaking directly to me. I've now recognized a pattern in my life: I often don't pay attention to my King.

Even if you are sure you are God's servant, if you are maturing in your commitment to Him, you may—like me and every Christian I know—fail to pay attention to your Master as a servant should. If you verbally say you are His servant, wait on His every whisper.

Servants Mind the Little Things

Richard Rogers (1550–1618) said, "We serve a precise God." Our Master cares about all the trivia of your life. Small things are important. A maturing Christian with a servant heart watches over conduct in the little matters of everyday life. If a tree is dying, you'll notice the trouble first in the tips of the little branches. *If your spiritual life is dying, you'll notice it in the little things.* As a maturing Christian, ask God to help build your relationship with Him in the little things.

M&M: *Ministry and Missions Moment*

One way to determine whether you are a servant is to look at your calendar. Do the items there show your servant actions? Are you busy serving God, waiting on Him just as a waiter or server in a restaurant tends to customers' needs? These may be good indications of servanthood, but I'd suggest another avenue: *Look for the little things.* What actions have you done today that went unnoticed, not recorded in your calendar or anyone else's? These things are likely to be the actions of a servant. As you actively engage in ministry and missions, think of how you can tell others about the true servanthood: life with Jesus.

Deeper Still: *Mystery Revealed*

A mystery that few understand is explained in Matthew 20:25–28. Jesus said, "You know that the rulers of the Gentiles lord it over them, and their high officials exercise authority over them. Not so with you. Instead, whoever wants to become great among you must be your servant, and *whoever wants to be first must be your slave*—just as the Son of Man did not come to be served, but to serve, and to give his life as a ransom for many." John gives us these words about servanthood near the end of the Bible: "Praise our God, all you his servants" (Revelation 19:5).

—— Study 7 ——

Courageous Faith

Martin Luther, born a son of a coal miner in Saxony, Germany, studied to be a lawyer. One day, in fear of God during a thunderstorm, he promised the Almighty he would become a minister. At the Augustine monastery, he suffered with *scrupulosity*—that is, a scrupulous attack on his own sins, confessing for hours each day every little sin he could remember and worrying about those he'd forgotten to confess. As a Bible study teacher at Wittenberg University, one day Luther found these words: "The just shall live by faith" (Romans 1:17). These words transformed him. He soon nailed his theses of these bold ideas to the Wittenberg church door for all to read. When ordered to recant, he courageously said, "I've been taken captive by the Word of God. Here I stand. I can do no other." Today we have Martin Luther's words from the hymn "A Mighty Fortress Is Our God" to remind us of his stand before the world. More than almost any other person, Luther demonstrated courageous faith as he did all he could to see that everyone had access to God's Word.

Twenty-first-Century Courageous Faith

As I write these words, it's the third anniversary of the deaths of three wonderful doctors and health workers in Yemen. On December 30, 2002, a gunman slipped into the Baptist Hospital in Jibla, Yemen, and killed Bill Koehn, Kathy Gariety, and Martha Myers. In just a few moments the three wonderful Southern Baptists passed into eternity. They gave their lives so people in Yemen could know who Jesus is.

In March 2003, a terrorist bomber killed a missionary in the Philippines. Bill Hyde was called "the big missionary with a bigger heart" full of love for Filipinos. Faithful unto death, he gave all so they could know Jesus. In March 2004, terrorists opened fire on Baptist missionaries David McDonnall and Karen Watson, along with Larry and Jean Elliott, as they drove their small truck in Iraq to survey a spot for water purification near Mosul. Their courageous faith had carried them to this war-torn country where they gave their lives for Christ.

January 9, 2006, was the fiftieth anniversary of the deaths of Nate Saint, Roger Younderian, Ed McCully, Peter Fleming, and Jim Eliot, whose wife Elizabeth continued to carry on his work among the Waodani people in the Ecuador jungle—faithful unto death.

More than 60 years ago, Cecil Dye wrote these words to his wife before going into the Bolivian jungle: "I don't believe we care so much whether this expedition is a failure.... We want God to get the most possible glory from everything that happens.... Perhaps more Christians would become more aware of their responsibility to lost men and less concerned over the material things of this life if the expedition failed and we lost our lives. Maybe they would pray more for the next group." Dye and four other New Tribes missionaries were killed and buried in the jungle. All set examples of how to live with courageous faith.

What Faith Is

God's Word says, "Faith is the substance of things hoped for, the evidence of things not seen" (Hebrews 11:1 KJV). *Substance* means faith is tangible, malleable matter of whatever is hoped— the solid, substantial, and visible witness—the physical evidence of the invisible. Since Adam and Eve, mortal humans have known what faith is, as they've risked their possessions, families, honor, reputations, and lives to live by faith in God.

Hebrews 11 offers examples of people who lived by faith, including kings, prophets, and prostitutes. People from all walks of life have relied on faith in God. All people have faith in something: themselves, another person, the law of gravity, the permanence of the earth...many things that cannot be trusted. However, those listed in Hebrews and those following that list, such as Martin Luther and others right up to the twenty-first century in which you live, have struck out on an adventure of faith, following Jesus to the end.

Abraham was 75 years old when God promised him, "I will make your name great, and you will be a blessing" (Genesis 12:2). When he was already well established in life, he obeyed God, left home, and went to "a land they knew not of" (Hebrews 11:8 KJV). The Hebrews writer describes other maturing Christians "who through faith conquered kingdoms, administered justice, and gained what was promised; who shut the mouths of lions, quenched the fury of the flames, and escaped the edge of the sword; whose weakness was turned to strength: and who became powerful in battle and routed foreign armies." God commended them for their faith, saying He "had planned something better for us so that only together with us would they be made perfect" (Hebrews 11:40).

A Giant Leap of Faith

The Swedish philosopher Søren Kierkegaard points out that courageous faith requires tremendous trust in the unknown and unseen. A mature Christian who trusts in God is like a man who moves to the edge of a giant precipice and then, leaning over the edge, takes a giant leap of faith. Such a leap requires courage. *It may take all you have inside you to abandon your will to His, but the greatest thing you give Jesus is reckless abandon.* As a maturing Christian, you release control of all your decisions, every detail of your life, to God's control, as you seek to understand His will.

Oswald Chambers, who died at age 47, possessed deep insights on courageous faith, which he passed along to us as a legacy. The following steps to courageous faith are based on his words:

1. Be ready to abandon all you seek; instead seek Jesus. The greatest words of Jesus to His disciples concerned abandon. Similarly, "when God has brought *us* into the relationship of disciples, we have to venture on His word; trust entirely to Him and watch that when he brings us to the venture, we take it" (italics added).

2. Pay attention to the source and He will look after the overflow. If you listen carefully and obey Jesus, He will take care of the details in miraculous ways.

3. Be patient and so utterly confident in God that you never question His ways or your waiting time. If all the world fell into a giant abyss except the small plot under your feet, would you still trust Jesus? If all your family died and your enemies surrounded you, would you still trust Jesus? A maturing Christian is patient, is confident, and never questions the way or the wait.

Though Abraham was known as the greatest patriarch of faith in the Old Testament, there came a day when his faith was tested to the maximum. God asked Abraham to sacrifice his precious son, Isaac, on an altar. In the British Museum of Art in London's Trafalgar Square hangs a painting of old Abraham with his hand over Isaac's eyes, so he won't see his father kill him. In Abraham's day, pagan cultures demanded child sacrifice, but God didn't demand it. He demanded Abraham's obedience, even to something that seemed repulsive. God provided a way to save Isaac, as He saved Abraham's heartache.

In her book, *I Lay My Isaac Down*, Carol Kent tells the horrible story of her son, a tender Christian young man, arrested and sentenced to prison (where he is today). Like any other broken-hearted mother, she cried, "Why?" However, she reflected on the story of Isaac, realized Abraham's broken heart, and saw God's perfect faithfulness. She and her son have now begun prison ministries, and as he serves these hard years, the family's faith has been strengthened.

My own pastor, Dr. Kirk Neely, suffered a time of faith testing. When his young adult son Erik died, he asked God, "Why?" Then one day on the beach, in an encounter with the Living God, his Heavenly Father told him to stop asking "Why?" and begin asking "What next?" He has since published a book that will help many others in their bereavement. (For help with your own bereavement or that of a friend, read Neely's *Strength for Today, Hope for Tomorrow: Our Shared Experience of Grief*, published by Baker Books.)

You may have read the poem that says your child is an arrow; you are the bow. You are bent and drawn taut so that the Archer can launch your children in the direction He wants them to go. God wants you to release your children, and you can do it *only through faith.*

In Mark 9, a father of an epileptic son showed his faith, saying "I do believe; help me overcome my unbelief" (v. 24). "If you have faith as small as a mustard seed, you can say to this mountain, 'Move from here to there' and it will move. Nothing will be impossible for you" (Matthew 17:20). Ask your Father for power to exercise the faith He's given you.

Why Maturing Christians Are Faithful

Finally, as a maturing Christian, you are faithful because God is faithful: Isaiah said, "O LORD, you are my God; I will exalt you and praise your name, for in perfect faithfulness you have done marvelous things, things planned long ago" (Isaiah 25:1). You can count on Him to do what He promised. "Have you not heard? Long ago I ordained it…now I have brought it to pass" (Isaiah 37:26). Faith keeps you going when all is lost. Faith keeps you loving your faithful God because you learned faithfulness from Him. Faith enables you to trust God in good times and bad, in rich times and poor, in times of peace—and even in times of terror. *You trust God, period.* Job, who had lost everything, and realistically knew he had *not* been blessed in his loss, shows incredible faith when he says, "Though he slay me, yet will I hope in him" (Job 13:15).

M&M: *Ministry and Missions Moment*

If you feel you don't have faith enough to witness the way you should or to step out in bold ministry, don't shrug your shoulders and say, "I don't have faith." Bring your mind and will to the deeps: concentrate—*not* on the lack of faith in your life, but on the *exact thing* that holds you back. Look it dead in the eye, and diagnose *how* it holds you back. Is it a fear? Is it a great loss you'll suffer if you step out in faith? Sue Carver, an Alabama Christian I admire, says this about trusting Christ with deep faith: "Whatever we are afraid of losing prevents us from following Christ, up close, in lock step. *Why can't we let go? Because we trust ourselves more than we trust God.*" And that truth is the essence of sin.

Deeper Still: *Mystery Revealed*

Praise God today because He is faithful. I've recognized this mystery as I've tried to be faithful in obeying Him: *God will usually call you to step out in faith on the days you're busy doing something else.* Ask Him to slow you down today. Take time to center your thoughts on God's will.

Pray that you'll have faith enough to trust Christ to handle the world. Start with a resolve not to think you must be responsible for all of life's tasks. Whatever worry you've had, that work can go on without you. God is big enough to handle it.

—— Study 8 ——

Solid Dependence on God

When a patient receives a bone marrow transplant, the donor's lifesaving blood cells flow into the patient's body, swimming from one body to the next. As the transfusion brings hope, it also brings unavoidable change. A battle rages inside the recipient's body. The new cells move through the body, confronting and conquering the cancerous cells. Like a no-nonsense landlord, the new cells claim ownership, kicking out the sick and tired old tenants. Painting and plastering with red, white, and plasma cells in the blood, they fix up the place, and a miraculous event occurs: healing. When the old occupants finally leave, so does the cancer. The process reminds me of the old hymn:

What can wash away my sin?
Nothing but the blood of Jesus;
What can make me whole again?
Nothing but the blood of Jesus.

Oh! precious is the flow
That makes me white as snow;
No other fount I know,
Nothing but the blood of Jesus.

In Him, we are new creatures. When God cleanses us, we can depend on Him!

How have you needed cleansing in your physical and spiritual life?

Praise God that you can depend on Him.

Depend on God's Peace and Safety

In 1998, I moved to Birmingham, Alabama, to house-sit for a friend's three-story home. My bedroom was bigger than my entire former apartment. I loved the space, the deck with a hot tub, and the balcony with private steps to the large den, but I was disturbed by things that go bump in the night. One night after hearing noises, going downstairs and searching every corner, I couldn't get back to sleep. Picking up my Bible, my eye fell on Isaiah 63:9, "In all their distress he too was distressed." As I read on, I found verse 14: "They were given rest by the Spirit of the LORD." I turned over, went to sleep and seldom heard the noises again. My heart was "fixed, trusting in the LORD" (Psalm 112:7 KJV). Isaiah says to God, "You will keep in perfect peace him whose mind is steadfast, because he trusts in you" (Isaiah 26:3).

You Don't Have to Fight the Battles

The Old Testament is filled with battles. Very often the Hebrews were told they didn't have to fight the battle themselves because God was with them. When Sennacherib, the king of Assyria, was ready to attack Israel, he laid siege on Jerusalem. Inside, God's people, who depended on Him, prayed and waited, just as we wait on God today. Sennacherib then sent envoys to ask: "On what are you basing your confidence?" King Hezekiah answered, "The LORD our God will save us" (2 Chronicles 32:10–11).

God tells us to wait on Him and He will save us. Hezekiah made a shrewd move: he stood firm where he was. As humans, we want to conquer everyone who attacks us. However, *you don't have to fight the battle*. God tells us to depend on Him, stand firm, and continue your work. Numerous times God's Word tells us of people who depended on Him, for example, "The widow who is…left all alone puts her hope in God and continues night and day to pray" (1 Timothy 5:5). Trust and continue.

Isaiah says, "Trust in the LORD forever" (Isaiah 26:4). How have your times of trusting God helped you mature as a Christian?

List some principles you have learned in this study that help you depend on Him.

Rely on God's Intangibles

Maturing Christians rely on the promises of God as if they were solid and tangible. When my husband slumped in the stadium seats, dying of a heart attack, a sudden presence of the Lord came over me, and I was impressed with the words "It is fitting." These three words revolved in my head, over and over. I remarked later to a friend that those words were strange, not usual words I use. They caused curiosity in my mind: How is this death fitting? Fitting what? Fitting *for what?* I looked up "fitting" in the dictionary: "Proper; matching a certain part or plan." I explored what God's plan was for me. Oswald Chambers says, "He is fitting us for whatever His work is for us to do." And fit He did! God reinvented my life; I've served in a different way ever since.

Because we're relying on the unseen intangibles, we don't fit into the world's traditions. God says, "You do not belong to the world, but I have chosen you out of the world" (John 15:19).

Can you look back on circumstance that demonstrated you depended on God? Write one account here:

Tell the story to an unsaved friend.

Undergoing a Paradigm Shift

When God infuses His Spirit into your life, He often offers you spiritual principles that parallel scientific principles—in your context—so you can better understand His communications with us. In Kohn's *The Structure of Scientific Revolutions*, he gives these three types of scientific phenomena: first, those that are already explained; second, those whose nature is understood but details need further articulation; and third, those that refuse to be assimilated into any understood paradigm.

When you, as a maturing Christian, hear God's voice, you're on the verge of a paradigm shift. You must be *strongly alert* to decide if this thought is valid. Is it already explained in God's Word? If you're familiar with God's Word, you know whether the idea is from God or from the world. No direct revelation from God disagrees with the Scriptures. If it agrees, you can trust it.

Second, if you know it's already explained in the Scriptures, some details may need further articulation. In other words, if general ideas apply to you, you need to flesh them out to get a solid footing. For instance, if a persistent idea crosses your mind to go to Iraq or China or Guatemala, then you, like Oswald Chambers, can remain "strongly alert," attuned to the Holy Spirit to fill in details. That may include reading newspaper articles about the country, looking up Internet information, or listening in church as mission teams talk about overseas missions.

Third, like scientific phenomena, some persistent ideas floating in your mind refuse to be assimilated into an understood paradigm. When the spiritual evidence isn't there, you may wonder if God would really ask you to step out on faith with a new extremely radical idea. As Christians mature, they measure God's call, trust His Word, read books by Christian writers whom they consider doctrinally correct, and seek advice of trusted ministers and solid Christian friends. If your sources are compatible with Scripture, move forward. (We will discuss more about being strongly alert in study 23.)

Peter says, "Scoffers will come, scoffing and following their own evil desires" (2 Peter 3:3). When they do, *be ready*. As you remain strongly alert, depend on Christ, ignore the scoffers, and stand firm.

M&M: *Ministry and Missions Moment*

Just as you depend on Him, God wants to depend on you as His faithful servant. Jesus said, "Be dressed ready for service and keep your lamps burning" (Luke 12:35). As you implement ministries in your community, remember: depend on God—nobody else.

Deeper Still: Mystery Revealed

Here's a great mystery in Christianity: *Trust in God makes you trustworthy.* As a maturing Christian, you learn to trust Him first; and you discover others can trust you, as you stand firmly for fairness and truth. Read Matthew 25:14–30 and meditate on your life as a dependable servant to your Master.

——— Study 9 ———

Order and Simplicity

A recent email included a news item about billionaire Michael Forbes' birthday party, which cost two million dollars (flying guests to an exotic place in South America) to celebrate. You may know others who amass wealth they'll never be able to use, or collect possessions in boxes ("collectibles") they never plan to open. Today's American has far too many worldly possessions, and Christians often fall into a worldly milieu before they realize it. Many immature Christians aren't good stewards, spending far too much time, energy, and money on shallow, frivolous celebrations.

On the other hand, Jesus gave us the most expensive celebration when He gave His life for our sins. We celebrate in our churches when we celebrate communion, a time to remember His sacrifice on our behalf. Maturing Christians begin by bringing their lives in order. They sacrifice certain worldly pleasures and excesses to live the Christian life more completely.

Indicators of a Spiritual Maturity

A simple life offers seven indicators of spiritual maturity:

1. Gentle Priorities

Rev. Duncan McGregor, a mentor and teacher, agreed with Oswald Chambers: "In ministerial training there should be less of the factory and more of the garden." Make an appointment on your calendar for times in the garden, times with children, and times with your prayer journal. Don't let anything preclude those appointments.

2. Financial Stability

Radio personality and financial expert Larry Burkett counseled with a pastor, who had never made more than $8,000 per year, about retirement. The inventory completed, he asked Burkett, "What will I be able to do?"

Burkett answered: "Anything you want! Do you want to adopt me?" The pastor had always spent less than he earned. He and his wife were also too busy serving God to go out and spend money. *The way you spend your money is a true indicator of how serious you are about following the simple life with God.*

3. Absence of Fads and Fashion

Christians spend vast amounts of money on clothes, conforming to present fads to fit in with current styles. Jesus said, "See how the lilies of the field grow? They do not labor or spin. Yet I tell you that not even Solomon in all his splendor was dressed like one of them. If that is how God clothes the grass of the field, which is here today and tomorrow is thrown into the fire, will he not much more clothe you, O you of little faith?" (Matthew 6:28–30). Keep your wardrobe classic and simple.

4. Comfort in Silence

God says, "Call on me and I will show you wondrous things ["remarkable secrets"] you do not know" (Jeremiah 33:3). He reveals His very heart in a whisper, a "still, small voice." In *What Happens When Women Pray*, Evelyn Christenson lists *silence* as one of the Six S's of Prayer. She gives an illustration of women at a lakeside retreat waiting for a trio to come across in a boat to sing. Five hundred women waited in silence at the water's edge. Something happened to the signal, and the trio kept waiting. Twenty minutes passed as Christenson and Mary, a testimony leader, fretted because of the silence. However, they found later that God had moved in the silence; many hearts were changed by His Spirit that night. Since God speaks softly in the silence, if you want to hear His voice, give Him a quiet time to speak. *One mark of mature Christians is that they're not afraid of silence.*

5. Daily Devotions

D. A. Ousley says, "Christian disciplines do satisfy our deepest longings (though they may not bring us money, worldly pleasure, or deliverance from pain and suffering). They are not just a secular self-help program of discipline; they are a program of change from the inside out." *Make a daily appointment with God.*

6. Devotion to Scripture

Ousley also says, "The person we know in prayer is the same person we meet on the pages of Scripture. Scripture also has a correction function." As we are told in 2 Timothy 3:16, the study of Scriptures offers us a foundation for stability in life. God's Word is a mirror into which we look to gain knowledge of ourselves. We find in the Scriptures the *significance* of our lives in God's eyes. Scripture is the source of spiritual nourishment, which gives us the framework to understand ourselves.

Read 2 Timothy 3:16, and complete the statements below:

All Scripture is...

And is useful (profitable) for...

Look back at your answers above. How have the Scriptures made an impact on your life in each of these ways?

7. An Air of Grace and Justification

Justification (by Christ's blood) gives us the possibility of new life, which must be lived out every day. Daily devotions engender sanctification, the growth of holiness within the Christian. Devotions include all the Christian life: cultivation of the virtues; discipline in prayer, public worship, Bible study, fasting, giving, and works of mercy. Also God's grace makes us holy and supports our own wills as we cooperate with Him. He gives us grace "both to will and to do of his good pleasure" (Philippians 2:13 KJV). God's grace trains us in the ways of holiness. *Apart from grace we can do nothing.*

8. A Balance of Life

In 1888, Robert van Deweyer suggested life could benefit from three basic balances: first, your use of money and other material resources; second, use of your time; and third, a balance within your heart. Stewardship of all three is a basic mark of spiritual maturity, and *stewardship is a part of the accountability to God* in an orderly life.

Richard Neibuhr, a twentieth-century theologian, regrets the fast-paced life of false values. He says, "We have produced a God without wrath, who brought man without sin into a kingdom without judgment through the ministrations of a Christ without a Cross." The cure for such a world is our allowing God to take charge of our lives, bringing purpose, order, and simplicity to us as we draw closer to Him.

M&M: *Ministry and Missions Moment*

You may be too busy doing the Lord's work to have time for the Lord. If that's the case, what can you do about it? Quit a ministry. Mentor someone to take your place. Seek God's face and favor on your knees. Ask advice from godly friends and church staff. *Don't minister out of guilt. Be absolutely controlled by God.*

Deeper Still: *Mystery Revealed*

Here's a mystery few Christians have uncovered: *Church service doesn't cause stress. You do that to yourself.* Today think about your need to live with order in your life. Meditate on Neibuhr's points: (1) the God of wrath and accountability; (2) your own sin; (3) the judgment of the kingdom of God; (4) the Christ of the cross. Decide on ways you can honor Him with your life.

Study 10
Advanced Moral Development

If you're considering a step of faith into a ministry arena, pause and look at your life purpose. Most of us have thought about long-term or short-term goals, but this is not a study about goals. Its purpose is to point you to direct confrontation with your purpose for being. Where do you stand on the ladder of obedience to God? Most of us haven't dreamed of the large place God has for us! Consider the shepherd David, who later became King of Israel. During the long Palestine nights, he must have looked into the heavens and considered the vastness of God's omniscience: "For as high as the heavens are above the earth, so great is his love for those who fear him" (Psalm 103:11). Have you contemplated the vastness of His love for you lately and the life work He intends for you to do? You reviewed in study 2 that you were created to do good works, "which God prepared in advance for us to do" (Ephesians 2:10). One way you know if you're at the point where you ought to be to fulfill what you were created to do is to measure your progress on a moral development ladder.

A man named Lawrence Coburg once investigated and defined the stages of moral development. (He worked at about the same time Erik Erikson was defining psychological development and Piaget was developing his cognitive development theory.) Here's a paraphrase of Coburg's stages of moral development:

Stage 1: Egocentric

A baby has an egocentric perspective: "I am at the center of the universe. Whatever is good for me is good. Period." If you've ever sat up all night with a crying baby or a toddler who just wants your attention, you understand this stage of development .

Stage 2: Simple Fairness

Most children have the simple fairness perspective. "You do this, and I can do that. What is done for one ought to be done for the other. What's mine is mine; what's yours is yours." For example, suppose you gave two children a bowl of m&m's to share. They will spend quite a while counting to be sure the candy is equally divided! Christians at stage 2 of moral development complain to God and fellow church members that their lives are unfair.

How have you seen stages 1 and 2 in action in your family or community?

Did those involved in these two stages mature later, or are they in process of maturing even now?

Why do you believe some people find it hard to outgrow these two moral stages?

Stage 3: Pleasing Authority

Most older, wiser children have this perspective. They do whatever it takes to please the person in authority. They make moral decisions to keep from getting punished. Some Christians obey God because they fear His punishment. They live in anxiety and terror as they try to serve God in local arenas.

Stage 4: Law and Order

Within this adolescent stage, all people abide by the same rules. Formal rules are codified, written for all to see. You've seen rules like these at swimming pools: "No running. No cannonballing. No glass containers around the pool." The law fits everybody. No exceptions.

When my granddaughter, Blakely, was three, she returned from Mom's Morning Out at her church saying, "Mimi, I know the rules!" Standing at attention, she recited loudly: "Rule number 1: No playing on the monkey bars! Rule number 2: Keep your hands to yourself...." She *knew* the law and order stage of moral development, though she might not have been able to *apply* it to her moral development.

Write a hypothetical example of an adult who lives in stages 3 or 4 of moral development.

Describe the behavior and resulting consequences:

Stage 5: Covenant

Adults and mature youth can comprehend this stage of trust building. In a Christian marriage, couples enter a covenant for life, based on devotion to another. According to Coburg, our US Constitution is the highest form of covenant living, with provisions for amendments. Perhaps most Christians live in this stage of moral development. They build a relationship with Christ, establishing a covenant with Him for life. However, from time to time, we may revert to stage 3 or 4 as temptation or stress infringe on our Christian faith and perseverance.

Stage 6: Golden Rule

The last stage of spiritual maturity is rarely achieved. Within it, humans exemplify the Golden Rule, doing to others what they'd have others to do to them. Coburg—even though he wasn't a Christian—listed Jesus as the best example of this stage, because He gave His life for others.

Different Stages Acted Out

My pastor, Dr. Kirk Neely, gave this example of a case he monitored as a counselor near Louisville, Kentucky. As a young man, aged 18, was shoveling snow, his neighbor, an elderly man, collapsed while also shoveling snow. Aware of the dangers of overexertion, the young man knew he had to get his neighbor to the hospital right away. Since he didn't have time to shovel his own car out, he immediately thought of an old, apparently abandoned, accessible car that had been sitting on his street for a week. He carried the man in his arms to the car, hot wired it, and took him to the hospital, where a nurse said he'd saved the life of the elderly man.

However, the owner of the abandoned car, realizing his car had been used, charged the young man with using a vehicle without permission. The young man was arrested and appeared before a judge, who made him serve six months in jail.

How does the snow-shoveling account illustrate several stages of moral development?

What behavior do you find as evidence that each character below was in a certain stage of development?

The young hero:

The car owner:

The judge:

The young man was acting at stage 6 of moral development. He treated the collapsed man as he wished to be treated. With super-human strength and quick thinking, he saved someone's life. However, the owner of the abandoned car was operating at stage 2 of moral development: "What's mine is mine; what's yours is yours." He felt it was not fair for the young man to take his car, no matter what the reason. The judge was operating from the perspective of stage 4 of moral development: Everyone should obey the law, as it is written. He lived strictly by the book; no exceptions.

Stage 6 people, like the heroic young man, break the law from above, thinking situations sometimes demand common sense when enforcing the law. Sometimes this is called situation ethics: the end justifies the means. On the other hand, stage 2 people, like the car owner, break the law from below: "If my company hasn't treated me fairly, then I can take money out of the till until we're even."

At what stage of moral development do you live your life?

Theorists tell us that spiritually mature people in stage 6 hate war; yet many full-time soldiers, who hate it the most, are in stage 6. They often volunteer for dangerous assignments because they have a spiritual bond with all humanity and, therefore, are willing to give their lives for others. (See study 23.)

Quaker leader John Woolman, a humble man in unbleached muslin suits, made free wills for many people. He required only one thing: that his clients state in their will that all their slaves would be set free when their owner died. One remarkable factor in John Woolman's life, at stage 6 in his moral development, is that he lived before the Revolutionary War. An active advocate for Native Americans, he also diagnosed pollution on Manhattan Island. No doubt this stage 6 hero was ahead of his time!

One might be almost sure that Lottie Moon and Mother Teresa were at stage 6 in their development, since they denied themselves food and rest while taking care of starving, poor people. Corrie Ten Boom, a survivor of cruelty in a World War II concentration camp, showed stage 6 behavior when she was able to shake hands with (and eventually forgive) the guard who'd mistreated her and indirectly caused her sister's death in prison. She wrote that she couldn't *will* her hand to touch his outstretched hand, but God enabled her to do it. Most of us must depend on Him to keep us stabilized in stage 6.

Most people never reach stage 6. Sometimes we muster an unselfish, caring spirit that leads to ministries of temporary compassion, but then we put the need out of sight, out of mind. For example, when a 2004 tsunami hit Indonesia and other countries, killing more than 100,000 people, large numbers of volunteers and money rose to the challenge. However, the unselfish outpouring soon faded. Can you think of other disastrous times when Christians initially demonstrated intense love for others, but later, their passion waned?

List occasions when you experienced the spirit of compassion of stage 6 in your community:

Give details of each occasion that showed the stage of moral development of those involved:

How did the knowledge of these occasions help form your personal sense of moral development?

Can you name someone you know who is a stage 6 Christian?

Can you move toward Step 6 without fear? As you close this study today, ask Him to give you courage to move deeper, still deeper into these steps.

M&M: *Ministry and Missions Moment*

Compare Philippians 2:3–4 with the Golden Rule: "Do unto others as you would have them do unto you" (Matthew 7:12 KJV).

According to Paul, what should be the Philippians' motivation?

How should you treat others? What kinds of activities should that involve?

List activities of a stage 6 Christian:

List other activities that come to mind when you think of the passages in the M&M Moment for today:

How could you personally become involved in such unselfish actions?

In your home or community, how could you become involved?

Describe at least one activity you dream of leading:

Deeper Still: Mystery Revealed

It took me years to recognize this mystery as I've lived the Christian life: *God loved you while you were in sin, but He'll call you to serve Him at a deeper level of morality than your past steps.* Ask Him to give you the courage to move to stage 6 and the character to maintain that level.

Unit 3

———————— ● ————————

CHALLENGES OF SPIRITUAL MATURITY

My lonely heart with feelings reels. A hole is there, O God.
I'm on a wild-goose chase into the neighborhood of nowhere.

Sometimes I cannot serve the world, nor can I serve You, Lord.
My business is busy-ness; a shallow, blind pursuit.

I know I miss the mark; each time I, false and fallow, fall
Apart, disjointed, off the track, I cannot see the lack.

Jesus, help me down, and deeper to Your heart I flow.
Deeper, softer path and clearer; leads to know, to know.

—— Study 11 ——
Misunderstood Feelings

All humans experience hormonal and emotional changes that affect their Christian maturity. As you mature, you find feelings can't be trusted; that which seemed logical or morally right turned out to be a fallacy and *just completely wrong*. Most people spend valuable time wondering what went wrong. The human perspective is faulty at best. Because we have built-in feelings that distort our focus, we need to be on guard. Feelings fight against everything spiritual: we become bored, discouraged, frayed, and tempted.

Feelings of Discouragement

Bobby Dagnel, a pastor, speaks about the feelings of a person who is frayed, who wants to climb back up from the end of the rope. Using Elijah, "the Iron Man of the Old Testament" as an example, he tells what happened when Elijah let his feelings discourage him. Elijah had come from a miracle at Mount Carmel, in which God brought down lightning from heaven and lit a fire on the altar. Then in 1 Kings 19, Elijah went into the Valley of Futility, Depression, and Despair. He began with fear (v. 3), which led to failure (v. 4), which led to fatigue (v. 5).

Feelings of Frustration

Here's what Elijah did to recover:

1. He took time off (1 Kings 19:3–5). Mature Christians usually plan downtime in an average day. In a life of order and simplicity (study 9), they eliminate the clamor that gives rise to emotional upsets. Taking time off does not have to be an exotic vacation in

Tahiti. It can be a quiet morning in the garden or an evening walk around the block.

2. He talked out his frustration with God (verses 9–10). Today's Christian has many options for counseling: a spouse or other family member, a pastor or church staff member, or a professional counselor.

3. He got life back into perspective (verses 11–12). Hearing "a gentle whisper," literally in Hebrew "a voice of quiet whispers," Elijah heard God speak with a still small voice. We still listen to that voice today. God is saying, "I may seem silent, but I'm still here. I'm still God."

4. He got back into the mainstream of life (verses 15–16). A mature Christian can wallow in self-pity for only so long; then you'll get up and get going! Once you've drawn aside for a walk with God and you've heard His voice, you're ready to serve Him again.

What is your favorite place for relaxation? Describe:

Describe the place where you habitually hear the "still, small voice of God."

What advice would you give people who fall into the trap of misunderstood feelings?

How would you describe the way maturing Christians can trust God regardless of the ups and downs of their feelings?

What has this study meant to you?

Feelings of Malaise

In Tucson, Arizona, a reporter asked psychiatrist Karl Menninger, "I feel I have a nervous breakdown coming. What should I do?"

Dr. Menninger said, "Walk out the front door of this office. Cross the railroad tracks, and find someone less fortunate than you. Help him."

Helping a needy person is a good cure for malaise, and it helps a maturing Christian get back on the right path. Even when we don't feel like it, we act out God's plan for our lives, according to the Scripture. As we offer Him our unselfish service, we'll grow deeper into the Spirit. Staying busy serving God and others keeps our feelings on track, aligned with His will. As we work for Him, we maintain the intimacy of a fellow worker (1 Corinthians 3:9).

Feelings of Dryness

Many people compare our relationship to God with marital love. When we first become Christians, we experience euphoria similar to a honeymoon. After a while, we're perplexed as we settle into a period of dryness. We ask God to speak, and sometimes He's silent. We're tempted to be unfaithful to Him, but we keep coming back, depending on Him. Finally, we're willing to love God so much that we serve Him unselfishly, no matter what His response.

We know His heart, and trust Him regardless. That kind of trust was God's aim all along, to lead us to mature love.

Reining in the Feelings

God's Word says, "There is a way that seems right to a man, but in the end it leads to death" (Proverbs 14:12; see also Proverbs 16:25). Maturing Christians are aware that feelings must be reined in by our wills, as we resolve to serve God, *even if we don't feel like it*. If left unbridled, feelings can take over our resolve, leading us astray. Paul describes people who've reverted back to walking in the flesh rather than the Spirit: "They are darkened in their understanding and separated from the life of God because of the ignorance that is in them due to the hardening of their hearts. Having lost all sensitivity, they have given themselves over to sensuality so as to indulge in every kind of impurity, with a continual lust for more" (Ephesians 4:18–19).

As you mature, look out for changing feelings! Decide ahead of time how you will handle them and relate to the feelings of others.

M&M: *Ministry and Missions Moment*

A spiritual counselor once told a pastor he was mentoring: "You'll never have warfare in your church or hurt feelings until you receive the…second member!" All humans have feelings that bring alternating euphoria and depression, false hope, and misunderstood words. Don't stop working with people or with God because you don't get "that happy feeling." One of the skills learned by maturing Christians is patient handling of (1) their feelings in their personal relationship with Christ and (2) others' feelings in their interpersonal relationships with Christians and non-Christians. Consider today all the people with whom you minister. While working with them, consider their feelings (aloof, sensitive, loving, afraid, insecure, etc.) and decide your own ethical approaches.

Deeper Still: *Mystery Revealed*

Here's a personal mystery: *Everyone, including you, has an Achilles' heel, a point at which you are vulnerable.* Sometimes you may not recognize your own weakness. When feelings run unbridled, you may live inconsistently and not seem like yourself. Identify your emotional or moral weaknesses and ask God to strengthen you as you dwell deeper in His Spirit.

—— Study 12 ——
A Busy Phone Line

I spent the week before my daughter's wedding day with last-minute trips to the caterer, the florist, the tuxedo shop, and the church—about 30 miles away. As happy as I was that Patsy was marrying Tim, a good Christian young man, I felt laden with responsibilities. My son, Jack, was away at college, but he said he'd be there to walk his younger sister down the aisle, taking the place of his dad, who had died a few years before. He teased Patsy, saying he had wanted to give her away since she was three!

To save money, I gathered blossoms from several friends who had large magnolia trees. Their luscious, creamy-white blooms and slick green leaves would make beautiful arrangements against the dark wood inside the church. After the rehearsal dinner the night before the wedding, we banked the podium and choir area with magnolias. As we left just before midnight, I felt tired but satisfied this would be the best wedding any bride had ever had!

The busiest day of my life arrived, and while Patsy's bridesmaids helped her dress, Tim walked with me to the sanctuary to be sure the flowers were intact. I almost fainted when we opened the door and felt a rush of hot air; and then I saw them: all the beautiful white flowers were black. Funeral black. An electrical storm during the night had disconnected the air conditioning system, and on that hot June day, the flowers had died.

Have you ever been to a sweaty wedding with black flowers? I don't think so!

Have you ever experienced a disaster like the black flowers at a wedding? Write about your experience, and share the story with a study partner (if you have one) or a family member.

How does your busyness interfere with your compassion for others?

Why do you think you stay busy most of the time?

Share your ideas on busyness with your study partner.

I panicked, knowing I didn't have time to drive back to our hometown, gather more flowers, and return in time for the wedding. Tim turned to me and asked, "Edna, can you get more flowers? If you can, I'll throw away these dead ones and put fresh flowers in these arrangements." I mumbled, "Sure," as he bebopped down the hall with his groomsman.

Alone in the large sanctuary, I was never so *unsure* of anything in my life. "Lord," I prayed, "please help me. I'm so angry. . . . Why did Patsy's daddy have to die? I'm all alone here. Why did she want to get married in Newberry—30 miles from home? If this were my own church in Clinton, I'd have friends to help me. I don't know anyone in this town. I'm tired of being the only one responsible for every detail. I've scrimped and saved every dime I could. . . . And now this. If I'd had enough money to buy florist flowers in the first place, this wouldn't have happened."

Spend a moment to analyze your method of praying. Which of the following do you usually do?
   a. Whine and complain to God, as I did
   b. Pray fervently, according to the urgency of the moment
   c. Ask and keep on asking; beg and keep on begging God to give you your requests
   d. Other:

Explain your usual prayer method to a study partner.

Suddenly aware of the urgency, I prayed, "Lord, I don't have time to whine. Help me find someone willing to give me flowers—in a hurry!" I prayed for four things: the blessing of white magnolias, courage to find them in an unfamiliar yard, safety from any dog that might want to bite my leg, and a nice person who wouldn't get out a shotgun when I asked to rip his tree to shreds! I didn't know if Newberry had a dog-leash law or whether drug dealers lived in the neighborhood, but I feared the worst.

Leaving the church, I saw magnolia trees in the distance. I approached a house with a giant magnolia tree and no dog in sight. I knocked on the door, and an older man answered. So far so good—no shotgun. He seemed happy to give me magnolias, climbing a stepladder and handing large boughs down to me. As I lifted the last armload into my car trunk, I said, "Sir, you've made the mother of a bride happy today."

"No, ma'am," he said. "You don't understand what's happening here, do you?"

"What?" I asked.

"You see, my wife of 67 years died on Monday. On Tuesday I received friends at the funeral home, and on Wednesday...." He paused. I saw tears welling up in his eyes. "On Wednesday...," he said, then swallowed hard, "...I buried her." He looked away. "On Thursday my out-of-town relatives went back home, and on Friday—yesterday—my children left for Greenwood, where they live."

I nodded.

"This morning," he continued, "I was sitting in my living room crying aloud. I miss her so much.... At least, for the last 15 years, as her health got worse, she needed me. But now...nobody needs me. This morning I cried aloud, 'Who needs an 86-year-old, wore-out man? Nobody!' I shook my fist. 'Nobody needs me!' About that time, you knocked, and said, 'Sir, I need you!'"

He grinned. "Do you know what I was thinking when I handed you those magnolias?"

"No," I said.

"I decided I'm *needed*. Why, I might have a flower *ministry*! At the funeral home, some caskets had no flowers. People need flowers at times like that. I have lots of flowers in the backyard. I might give them to hospitals, churches—all sorts of places. I'm going to serve the Lord until the day He calls me home!"

Read Isaiah 43:1–10. Verses 1–2 and 10 explain that God has chosen you to be His _____ or _____ .

Write here ways you may become those two things for Him:

What does God promise (vv. 4–5) He will do to prepare and encourage you in ministry He has called you to do?

According to God's Word, why should you never fear?

God Hears You When You're Hurting

I've often thought of James Smith, the widower whose heart was breaking on Patsy's wedding day. God was certainly aware of his pain. He saw His child—at 86—crying as he grieved. God covers us with overwhelming love when we hurt.

God Calls You When You're Busy

To tell the truth, if someone had said, "Edna, there's a man near the church who needs encouragement," I would have said, "No way. It's Patsy's wedding day, I'm too busy. Not today!" I believe God said, "I want to help James, but he's having such a pity party that I can't get through to him. Whom could I send to cheer him.... Oh, there's Edna, two blocks away. I've given her the gift of encouragement. She could help James, but she's also self-centered today. All she can think of is Patsy's wedding; she wants it to be the best. Yes, she's proud of herself, busy with responsibility for all details. She'd never stop fussing over the wedding to minister to James, a stranger.... Now, let me see...how can I get Edna to help James?"

God looked around, and His almighty eye fell on the magnolias in the sanctuary. Bloop. "That one's dead." Bloop, bloop. "Those two are dead." Bloop, bloop, bloop.... Through those dead flowers, God got me out of the church and into the world—even on the busiest day of my life!

Recall a time in your life when your need and your ministry coincided (your need led to a situation where you were able to minister to someone else) as Edna's did. Write your memory of the situation here:

Share this experience with someone later.

Can you think of opportunities you may have missed because you were too busy?

How are you handling such times today? This month? This year?

The Problem with Internal Noise

Most of the time you may feel you can't answer God's call because you have too many activities in your life screaming for attention. Thomas Kelly, in *A Testament of Devotion*, says we have an internal problem. As you read these words, you may be thinking, *I know: external noise leads to my internal problem.* No, Kelly says it's *internal noise.* In our minds is a fighting to be heard, as if we have a committee of selves and each self wants to have a say in the meeting. This cacophony leads to a disorganized, chaotic mind playing catch-up with life. *Each one of us needs a brain with a strong chairman of the committee. It must be the Living Christ who quiets us.* Quakers call this "centering prayer." It is a yielding to God's whisper.

M&M: *Ministry and Missions Moment*

After the wedding, the nearby church ministered to James Smith's needs. How would you do follow-up ministry in a similar situation? Is God leading you to step into a radical arena of ministry, but you've been (a) too busy to think about it; (b) whining about the imperfections in your life, family, or job; (c) dragging your feet because of doubt; or (d) afraid of stepping out into that radical arena, even though you know He's calling you? Read Isaiah 43 again, focusing on verses 1–2, 4–5, 8, and 10. *Act on the wisdom God shows you.*

Deeper Still: *Mystery Revealed*

Here's a spiritual principle I've discovered, one that was a mystery to me for many years: *There are hurting people, like James, all around you every day.* Ask God to show you who they are. Pray that He'll make you alert to needed lifestyle changes that are a part of His mysterious will for your life.

—— Study 13 ——
False Sense of Humility

She came into our state Woman's Missionary Union® office, looking for help. "I am the new leader of Women on Mission® in my church," she said shyly.

"Great!" I said. "I'll be glad to help you. We have many resources for women." I gave her a magazine, a resource kit, a how-to manual, and several other resources.

Her lip quivered. "I just don't know if I can be a leader."

"Why don't you ask your pastor's wife to help you?" I suggested.

She hesitated.... "I *am* the pastor's wife."

"How long have you been the pastor's wife?"

"Over 40 years."

"And you've never led a group of women before?"

"No."

I confess I wanted to shake her and say, "How could you have been his wife and never helped him with women's leadership?" Then I softened. She was clearly a shy lady, and leadership of a large crowd might bother her.

"How many women do you think will come to these meetings?"

"In a good month?"

"Yes."

"Usually we have…maybe…four or five."

That did it. My voice raised a few decibels: "And you've *never* led a few women in 40 years?"

Regaining patience, I encouraged her to step out in faith, promising to come several times over the next year to help her. After she left, I sat down and contemplated why godly women like her in the

Church sit for years without launching into a challenging position of leadership and service.

Whether you like it or not, God's people are how God has chosen to change the world. If you are reading this book, chances are you're a godly woman. If you shrink back from admitting you're godly, then consider these points:

You Are Godly Because...

1. Godliness (righteousness) is a gift. You don't get godly by being good. "For it is by grace you have been saved, through faith—and this not from yourselves, it is the gift of God—not by works, so that no one can boast" (Ephesians 2:8–9).

2. You become godly by accepting Jesus into your heart. If you've done that, a godly Spirit lives within you. "For it is with your heart that you believe *and are justified*, and it is with your mouth that you confess and are saved. As the Scripture says, 'Anyone who trusts in him will never be put to shame'" (Romans 10:10–11). As you repent of wrongdoing, believe in Him as Savior, and ask Him to help you live as a Christian, you will, step by step, release your old life dedicated to self and shame, growing secure in your stronger, godly life dedicated to Him.

3. You're blameless and holy in God's sight. "For he chose us in him before the creation of the world to be holy and blameless in his sight" (Ephesians 1:4). If you can't forget the wrong things you've done and accept Christ's forgiveness for them, you are failing to receive the greatest blessing of a Christian: living a shame-free, guilt-free life.

4. Because you're holy in His sight, you're chosen as a witness. "You are my witnesses...whom I have chosen" (Isaiah 43:10). A woman who spent the night in a bar last night is not going to tell the world about Jesus. She won't witness. You will, if you are a Christian, whether it's a good or bad witness. Being aware of your witness opens your eyes to your *holiness* as well as your responsibility to give a righteous witness.

5. When you accept yourself as Jesus sees you, you'll like yourself more and more. "To the saints…the faithful in Christ Jesus: Grace and peace to you from God our Father and the Lord Jesus Christ" (Ephesians 1:1–2). Accept yourself as a saint, a faithful Christian. As you read His words now, allow His peace to come into your heart completely, as His grace continues to sanctify you (making you increasingly more acceptable in His sight). Perhaps you've done this many times before. You can't accept His peace in one moment, because it's recurring, part of the sanctification process. Christians practice instant acceptance of His peace *daily* on the road to spiritual maturity.

6. When you like yourself, you can begin to become more Christlike, with divine love, grace, and confidence. "I always pray with joy because of your partnership in the gospel from the first day [of your salvation] until now, being confident of this, that he who began a good work in you will carry it on to completion until the day of Christ Jesus" (Philippians 1:4–6). As a Christian, you are a partner in the gospel. You, like Paul, can be confident that He's completing you as you accept His grace.

7. Every Christian is given the same measure of faith. How you develop that which He's given you is up to you. "Think of yourself with sober judgment, in accordance with the measure of faith God has given you" (Romans 12:3). In Greek, it is not the indefinite article, which in English reads: "*a* measure of faith," but the definite article "*the* measure of faith," meaning a definite amount God gives to all Christians. Don't judge yourself flippantly; hold your measure of faith in reverence. Pray for His instruction on how to exercise and use it.

8. You're important to God. "Don't you know that you yourselves are God's temple and that God's Spirit lives in you?"

(1 Corinthians 3:16). "Sing, O Daughter.... Be glad and rejoice with all your heart.... The LORD your God is with you, he is mighty to save. He will take great delight in you...he will rejoice over you with singing" (Zephaniah 3:14, 17). What is God singing over you today? Rejoice that you, His temple, are an important part of His world.

9. Your niche in God's plan is important to Him. If you don't fill that part in His plan, He'll reluctantly find someone else to do it...or your act of service may go undone. Not only are you a part of the Creator's overall plan for the world, but also you have specific tasks to do in His plan. Review Ephesians 2:10: "For we are God's workmanship, created in Christ Jesus to do good works, which God prepared in advance for us to do." Did you see two important words in that last sentence: *in advance?* Since God planned ahead what He wanted you to do in His kingdom, your job is to find out exactly what His plan is, and then to fulfill your task *already determined by His will.* "Be very careful, then, how you live—not as unwise but as wise, making the most of every opportunity.... Therefore do not be foolish, but understand what the Lord's will is" (Ephesians 5:15–16).

10. God has designed your unique DNA, life position, and opportunities for service. How you accept your uniqueness is your choice. David describes God's design of your life: "You created my inmost being; you knit me together in my mother's womb. I praise you because I am fearfully and wonderfully made.... All the days ordained for me were written in your book before one of them came to be" (Psalm 139:13–14, 16). Paul also gives us a model for our attitude about our life's position: "I have learned to be content whatever the circumstances. I know what it is to be in need, and I know what it is to have plenty. I have learned the secret of being content in any and every situation, whether well fed or hungry, whether living in plenty or in want" (Philippians 4:11–12).

One of the mysteries of Christianity is the hidden reason God has placed you in a certain situation. He makes no mistakes. You're where you are because of His permissive will and His active purpose. Through His Word, daily prayer, and Christian training, preaching, and fellowship in a local church, He'll reveal his purposes. *Nobody can fulfill the kingdom niche God planned for you in exactly the way you would, because He's created you uniquely suited to witness and give glory to Him in exactly the spot where you are.*

As Clarence said in the Christmas movie, *It's a Wonderful Life,* "When one person's not in place, it leaves an awfully big hole."

List some of your unique traits/opportunities below:

Things I've inherited from family DNA that I wish I didn't have:

Ways I can use inherited traits to serve God and bless others:

Things I've inherited that are blessings:

Ways I can show my thanksgiving for these traits:

A position I'm in now that I wish I weren't in:

Ways I can serve God and bless others through this unique position:

A position I'm in, for which I thank God:

Ways I can serve God and show my thanksgiving for this position:

New avenues of service I've just recognized:

11. You need to focus on the spiritual race before you. Allow no false humility, pride, tradition, "Mama," other people, or things to get in the way of following His will. Sometimes you and I—even spiritually mature Christians—can get sidetracked as we fulfill God's plan for our lives. In study 14, you'll look at things that distract you from discovering the knowledge hidden within the mystery of Christ. "You were running a good race. Who cut in on you and kept you from obeying the truth? That kind of persuasion does not come from the one who calls you" (Galatians 5:7). "Since we live by the Spirit, let us keep in step with the Spirit. Let us not become conceited, provoking and envying each other" (Galatians 5:25–26). Whatever others do around you, forget it. Move on, as you focus on the race before you. You are godly. Act accordingly!

Many mature Christians hesitate to step up to the plate with the task God has given them, such as leading or mentoring, because years ago they were taught that pride, one of the seven deadly sins, was unlovely, or even harmful to one's character. When they were children, they heard "Children should be seen and not heard,"

"You need to be taken down a peg or two," and "You're getting too big for your britches." Until about 1970, any self-esteem in a child in the family was stamped out as soon as possible. No family wanted a child with self-esteem!

Consequently, these children grew up to be Christians who take a backseat in ministry. Some of them have the idea they have nothing to offer. They're willing to let someone lead who's better educated, wealthier, or more powerful. They're intimidated by self-assured baby boomers and/or younger people. I know, because I am one of those from the silent generation who've reluctantly had to overcome a background of insecurity to lead others. Although spiritually mature Christians have a wealth of information and experience, they feel inadequate to tell others how to live their lives. They take the path of least resistance, not recognizing their talent or responsibility to witness, lead, or mentor. You cannot—you must not—sit and do nothing!

Remember, no matter when you were born, *it's His plan to use godly (redeemed, sanctified by Christ's Spirit) Christians, and you're it!* False humility has no place in the confident life of a Christian.

In which era were you born? (Dates vary slightly, depending on the researcher.) Circle your answer:

a. **The Builder Generation:** Pre–World War II; Victrola music, crystal sets, 78 records

b. **The Silent Generation:** 1939–1945; radio, TV emerged in teens, hi-fi, 33 $1/3$ albums

c. **Baby Boomers:** 1946–1964; television, 45 rpm records, eight-track tapes

d. **Baby Busters (Generation X):** 1965–1979; cable TV, audio-cassettes, videotapes, computers

e. **The Millennial Generation:** 1980–present; email, palm pilots, iPods, CDs, DVDs

How did your generation's method of communication affect your lifestyle?

How did your early lifestyle affect your confidence to witness, lead, or mentor?

According to the next "Deeper Still: Mystery Revealed," how can you renew your view of pride and use it for God's glory?

M&M: *Ministry and Missions Moment*

Read Ephesians 1:8–9. In what way has God lavished His grace on you with all wisdom and understanding? Using the Scriptures provided in the "You Are Godly Because…" principles, write your own personal "I Am Godly Because…" list. Ask God to show you how to personalize these general principles to apply to the unique circumstances of your life. What things in your life bring you unashamed pride, as you point to His love for you? How can you use those to witness and minister to others?

Deeper Still: *Mystery Revealed*

Here's today's mystery of the Christian life: *Since godly Christians have abhorred pride as the worst deadly sin, you need to renew your view of it, use it for God's glory, and recognize it as a necessity for your ability to witness and lead.* Ask Him to show you how to tame your pride and have the confidence to be a servant leader.

———— Study 14 ————
Distracted and Sidetracked

When my friend Elizabeth invited me to her bridal luncheon, I began counting the days till I could celebrate the occasion. I marked the date in red on my kitchen calendar so I wouldn't forget it. One Saturday morning my father called, saying, "They're building a new state park over near McCormick. Your mother and I are going to drive over to see what it looks like. Want to go?"

I said yes, of course. Dressing quickly, I jumped into their car a few moments later. After about an hour's drive, I remembered: *Today was the date for Elizabeth's bridal luncheon.* It was then too late to turn around, dress, and arrive on time for the luncheon. My feelings of guilt and stupidity spoiled my time with my parents at the state park. With no cell phone or other way of canceling my plate at the luncheon, I felt trapped watching new roads, park equipment, and bathhouse installations. I later wrote a sincere note of apology, but our friendship never seemed the same. My distraction had spoiled a relationship.

A Rushed Heart

One of the characteristics of spiritual maturity is a Christian's ability to focus on the peace of Christ and the task at hand without distraction. Your heart isn't rushed. You don't feel like the white rabbit in Lewis Carroll's *Alice in Wonderland*: "No time to say 'Hello'—'Goodbye!' I'm late, I'm late, I'm late!" A spiritually mature Christian has the God-inspired spirit of calm, even in situations filled with stress and chaos. The mind of peace and focus has a confidence that is evident in stressful situations.

List a few things that might sidetrack you from having the mind of Christ:

Read the following Scriptures. Beside each, write in your own words what the verse says about living in harmonic relationship with other Christians.

1 Corinthians 1:10

Philippians 2:3

Philippians 4:2

1 Peter 3:8

2 Thessalonians 2:2

Read these verses again, and reflect how you can "be of one mind, not distracted."

Memorize at least one verse, and after a few days, write here how your life has been changed by God's Word:

A Careless Crop

Read Luke 8:4–15. In a parable about a farmer, Jesus describes you. Each of us will fall into one of these categories: the hard ground that was trampled on, the rock, the thorny ground, and the good soil. If you are one whose path is trampled on, the birds (evil influences) steal the seed of the Word of God. In other words, you let Satan distract you so much that you carelessly ignore God's Word, never becoming a believer.

If you're in the second category, you are like a rock. Look carefully at verse 13. How do these people accept God's Word? How sad that they are joyous, but His Word does not take root. Christian statistician George Barna says one of today's tragedies is that Christians don't allow God's Word to take root and change their worldly behavior. It makes no difference in their lives. Since rocky soil can't allow deep roots, your religion will be shallow, and when dry periods of testing come, you'll carelessly lose touch with God and fall away from Him.

If you're in the third category, you allow life's thorns—worries, riches, and pleasures—to choke God's Word. You're distracted by the negative and positive influences of postmodern culture on your life. Notice God's sad commentary on this kind of careless person: "*they do not mature*" (v. 14).

If you're in the last category, you have "a noble and good heart" and you do three things: hear God's Word, retain it, and persevere to produce a crop. Your life is fertile, productive, growing in relationship to the sower, God Himself. This category is filled with people who are *not careless* with the Word of God. They are maturing Christians.

Read 2 Corinthians 8:10–12. What does Paul say you must do after your mind is willing?

Write words you find in these verses that show the church at Corinth had been sidetracked:

Identify one practical activity you could do to overcome rushing and careless behavior?

Share with a close friend or study partner how this study applies to your life.

A Messy Universe

Sometimes you may be distracted by a messy world: your husband drops his dirty socks in the living room; your children spill hot cereal on the floor; your bills arrive early this month and are scattered all over the desk or bulletin board in the kitchen until you have time to pay them. You can't dust for the clutter. At work your supervisor demands you clean up your workspace, but if you do, you can't find anything. You could serve God if everything in this world was clean and orderly.

However, the world itself is not orderly. Scientists who study it even refer to their scientific theories as "probabilities in a messy universe." Sometimes things don't fit. Even in your spiritual life, you run upon ideas or circumstances that don't seem to fit your worldview or your established lifestyle. At other times you recognize evil in your path; it distracts you for a time—it may even sidetrack you for years—but you don't have the time or the heart to get back on track.

A famous pastor once told our group: "There is no such thing as a nonmess!" In other words, the world will always be in a mess; it will never be perfect. You can't let that be your excuse for not fulfilling God's will for your life—or for failing to share your knowledge of His will with your world. No matter what tries to derail you today, look it straight in the eye, saying, "Get out; I refuse to live in a mess. I will not sit on the sidetrack, victim instead of victor!"

Your eyes and ears need to focus on Christ. *Listen to Him with two ears open and one mouth closed.* "Turn my eyes away from worthless things; preserve my life according to your word" (Psalm 119:37).

M&M: *Ministry and Missions Moment*

S. A. Chambers said, "We must not wait until every church is lighted with an elegant chandelier before we send the lamp of God's word to the nations that sit in darkness." You can't wait till furniture is dusted, toys are picked up, and personal issues are settled before you focus on Christ. Barbara Curnutt, a Georgia executive whom I admire said, "Neither crises, conflicts, nor criticisms will defeat us when our mind is stayed on Him." Decide this week on actions of ministry and/or missions you can do, in spite of the mess.

Deeper Still: *Mystery Revealed*

Here's a mystery revealed for mature Christians today: *Taking the scientific principle of a messy universe to the level of a spiritual truth, Satan uses the messy universe to distract you. Mature Christians recognize him, even in the midst of chaos, because he is the master of chaos.*

——— Study 15 ———
Potholes in the Road

When I was a little girl, my parents gave my brother and me each a bicycle for Christmas. On the first day of practice, after I had skinned my knees falling several times in cracks or potholes in the cement drive, our father explained: "Edna, when you're riding a bike, you must keep on pedaling or else you fall. You can't keep your balance when you stop pedaling. Don't stop to avoid every crack in the cement." Like riding a bicycle, moving down the road to Christian maturity requires perseverance. On this spiritual journey, you can't move forward while standing still, afraid of every trauma in life. If you stop over every crack in the road, you fall and fail. To develop spiritually, you must use caution, keep your balance, avoid the potholes, hurdle the cracks, and—*above all—pedal forward.*

Use Caution

As one moving toward Christian maturity, you must watch out for potholes. Discouraging times can cause gaping holes on the journey, as can a family member with a nagging tongue or a friend with the "gift of criticism." Be aware that Satan lurks behind every turn, and he appears often on the journey when opportunity exists. He is the master of skinned knees and broken dreams. "Be self-controlled and alert. Your enemy the devil prowls around like a roaring lion looking for someone to devour. Resist him, standing firm in the faith…. And the God of all grace…will himself restore you and make you strong, firm and steadfast" (1 Peter 5:8–10).

Deeper Still

Do you believe "Discouraging times cause gaping holes"? Why or why not?

What discourages you?

Write 1 Peter 5:8–10 in your own words, as it applies to your life.

Recognize the Signs

Most accidents happen when people are not watching for signs of danger. We Christians don't have a good track record for keeping out of trouble. We might set the goal "Never fail," but there's no way to reach that goal in this life. The quest for spiritual maturity is endless. Like the road to a good marriage, it's always in need of road work to patch up our Christian character. However, you can recognize the times when you tend to fall into the potholes of life:

- When you're hungry
- When you're lonely
- When you're tired
- When you're busy
- When you're sad (bereaved, depressed, loss of job, etc.)
- When you're tempted
- When you're ignorant of
  a. God's Law/His Word
  b. Facts about what God is doing in the world
  c. Christian opportunities/options/choices

Eve and Christ were tempted with food. Hunger, and all the other circumstances in the list above, identify a condition when you're off guard, inclined to fall into a pothole.

Potholes are full of dirt. On your spiritual journey, you call it *sin*. Read the following verses prayerfully, thinking about how Christians might react to sin: "How, then, can they *call* on the one they have not believed in? And how can they *believe* in the one of whom they have not heard? And how can they *hear* without someone preaching to them? And how can they *preach* unless they are *sent*?" (Romans 10:14–15, italics added).

Write the action verbs above in chronological order, according to the way Christians should react to sin in the world.

1.

2.

3.

4.

5.

Beside each one you've listed, write what you can do to send someone who will preach so sinners can hear, believe, and call on Christ for salvation.

Prevent Potholes

Each year farmers spray a preemergent herbicide to prevent weeds from sprouting. Roadway crews also spray a preemergent herbicide to prevent weeds from growing in little cracks in a tar-and-gravel or asphalt road. Potholes can be avoided by destroying weeds that uproot the road. Last Thanksgiving my pastor said that *gratitude reduces stress* and other weeds in our minds and hearts. It's a weed killer inside the heart. If your heart is full of gratitude, then no room exists for despair, anxiety, or hatred—and other potholes on the path to Christian maturity. A thankful heart is fertile ground for stability of soul, without the weedy emotional traumas of life. You can prevent potholes with thanksgiving.

We are blessed to live in America, the only country in the world that has a holiday of Thanksgiving to God. George Washington declared it a national holiday in 1789, Abraham Lincoln made it officially the last Thursday in November, and maturing Christians can make it official every day of their lives!

Recognize Pothole Blessings

A maturing Christian knows disasters can be blessings. Early in our marriage, Snow enjoyed plowing a small farm our extended family owned just outside the city. One day when a helper, Sam, was driving our tractor, he ran into an underground rock, breaking the shaft. That tractor was a special "Golden Jubilee" antique Snow had treasured. He was devastated, feeling we'd never fix the tractor in time for planting spring crops. We had no money to repair it. He prayed with Sam, who had only prayers and no money either, that God would find a solution before spring. After a few fretful days of worry, Snow checked with our local insurance company, who informed him they had a standard refund for such a vehicle accident. The amount would cover the cost of repair. What he had considered a disaster had become cause for thanksgiving. When Snow carried the money to the farm to see if Sam knew a repairman, he found him grinning. He'd just repaired the tractor. It looked like new. The insurance refused to take back their check, and so we experienced a double blessing from God! We learned we could trust God completely, even in dire circumstances.

Paul says, "So then, just as you have received Christ Jesus as Lord, continue to live in him, rooted and built up in him, strengthened in the faith, as you were taught, and overflowing with *thankfulness*" (Colossians 2:6–7).

Follow Five Paths to Spiritual Maturity

The road to spiritual maturity does not go straight upward, like a growth chart in a corporate marketing department. It does spiral ever outward, but also ever deeper and wider with understanding, in deep rest as it reaches toward the heart of God. As you veer off the path, God nudges you back. As you ask for help, He lifts you up onto the road again. "Your love is ever before me" (Psalm 26:3). Psalm 25:4–5 has a good road map to *deeper-still* maturity: "Show me your ways, O LORD, teach me your paths; guide me in your truth and teach me, for you are God my Savior, and my hope is in you all day long." When you allow God to

1. show you His ways,
2. teach you His path,
3. guide you in His truth,
4. be your God and Savior, and
5. give you hope,

you can stay on the path 24/7, maturing your Christian character. You're able to see His goodness and mercy, which follow you all the days of your life, and you'll dwell in the house of the LORD forever (Psalm 23:6).

On the spiral on this page, place "Birth" at the top and "Heaven" at the bottom. Then add significant times of spiritual growth (salvation, church attendance, ministries, etc.) at appropriate spots on your maturity spiral.

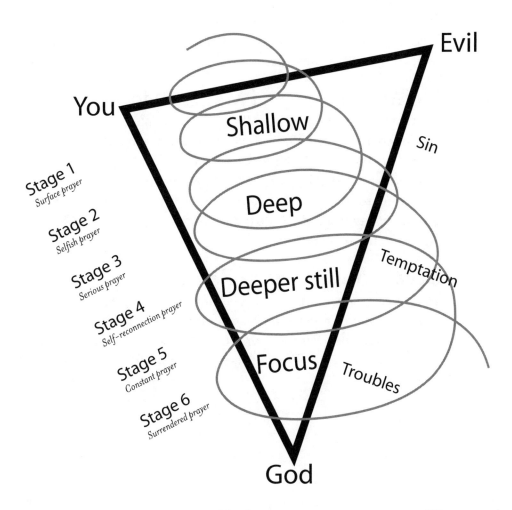

Add a few potholes you've experienced in your Christian walk.

Label the left side of the spiral with the five paths to spiritual maturity, in any order you wish. Use this spiritual growth spiral as your Christian growth autobiography, adding other milestones in the future.

Keep Pedaling

Take the advice my father gave me: keep pedaling. Don't be discouraged when you fall into a pothole. Remember, the road to spiritual maturity always needs road work.

M&M: *Ministry and Missions Moment*

"So that they may have the full riches of complete understanding in order that they may know the mystery of God, namely Christ, in whom are hidden all the treasures of wisdom and knowledge" (Colossians 2:2–3). You are a treasure, and hidden within your heart is a treasure box. *Fill your treasure box with the preemergent herbicide of gratitude.* Meditate today on this text, thanking God for the full riches of a grateful heart.

Deeper Still: Mystery Revealed

Brother Lawrence said, *"Most of us are atheists half the time. When we're doing our own thing, we forget God is there."* Meditate on this mystery today. Be aware of your atheistic times, when your mind is not centered on God. Be alert to the potholes that might destroy your inner peace.

Unit 4

———— • ————

GROWING SPIRITUALLY MATURE

It's just a small, small seed, a bud; the miniscule, it opens.
The life unformed. And we must wait, to linger in the deep.

To lie before we sleep. To die before we reap. —And then
A metamorphosis. God grows a spark deep in the dark.

And with the company I keep, I'm crossing all the barriers,
Starting, stepping, bursting, blooming, faster now I grow.

In leaps of hope I leave my hearth at home at dawn and then
I reach the top, the last step on the last frontier—home true.

——— Study 16 ———
Lingering in His Presence

A road construction company hired a man to paint lines on the highway. The first day he painted a mile and a half of highway, for which he was commended. The second day he completed only half a mile. On the third day he completed only an eighth of a mile.

When asked why his work decreased each day, he answered, "I kept getting further and further away from the paint bucket." The resource for the painter's work was in the paint bucket, yet he wasn't near enough to it to accomplish what he was called to do. Your spiritual work also suffers when you're too far away from your source. *If you want to take leaps in your maturation journey, one of the most important things you can do is to stay close to your spiritual source, the Holy Spirit*. Take God's paint bucket with you as you go. Invite the Holy Spirit to accompany you every step of the way.

Spend Time with Jesus

God's Word gives examples of mature Christians who spent time with Jesus. "So they went and saw where he was staying and spent that day with him" (John 1:39). To know Him intimately, spend time near Him. In one of my favorite hymns are these lines: "I love to tell the story; for those who know it best / seem hungering and thirsting to hear it, like the rest." Maturing Christians can't get enough of the presence of God in their lives. Their lives reflect an enthusiasm for lingering in His presence. They read His Word, pray constantly, and go to church so they don't miss any chance of learning more about Him. I've heard many Christians say, "I'm regular in church attendance because I don't want to miss one opportunity to commune with Him," or "On my way to church, I think, *This may be the time the power of the Holy Spirit comes down in full manifestation!* I want to be there when God shows up!" I am one of those people. I want to see the Lord as Isaiah did: "high and exalted, and the train of his robe filled the temple" (Isaiah 6:1–8). If I want to mature my faulty Christian walk, I need to face that I'm often inconsistent. I must *constantly* build the relationship with Him.

Build a Deeper Relationship

The unique characteristic of Christianity is that Almighty God wants a relationship with you. No matter how many years you've known Him, there's always one more area in which you can know Him better. He continues to unfold His heart, mind, and soul to you, year after year, in a deeper way as you mature in your relationship. If your husband said habitually, "Honey, I love you, but I can't be here tonight or tomorrow…or all next week," would you think his "I love you" was sincere? You'd believe he loved you if he wanted to linger in your presence. It's as simple as that. Your spouse builds a deeper relationship of trust as years go by. If you sincerely love God, you'll linger in His presence, building a relationship that deepens over time. No other activity with work, community, or even family will keep you from His presence. You'll discipline yourself to fulfill other obligations efficiently so you save time for Him. As you work through the following activity, analyze your enthusiasm for lingering in His presence and showing others His presence as well.

Take the Name of Jesus with You

On the next page, space and headings for two columns are provided. In the left column, list things you've done lately to show your devotion to Jesus. List times you've spent in Bible study, prayer, or Christian education. In the second column list times you've taken the name or the words of Jesus with you to share what you've learned in your contemplative time with Him.

Times of Lingering in His Presence	Times of Showing His Presence to Others

Be Mary and Martha

I used to think there were two kinds of Christians, the "be still and know" Christians, like Mary of Bethany, who sat at Jesus's feet basking in His presence, and the "get up and go" Christians, like her sister Martha, who *interrupted the Savior* to complain about the work she had to do in the kitchen (Luke 10:38–42). I now believe you can't be a Martha, in service for Him, unless you are a Mary, willing to take time to fill your heart with His *presence*, His *precepts*, and His *power*. Be both!

Seek His Presence

David said, "My heart says of you, 'Seek his face!' Your face, LORD, I will seek" (Psalm 27:8). Something inside every human heart, a yearning for the Creator, urges every person to seek God's face.

One way a maturing Christian seeks the Lord's face is through prayer. We "come before his presence with thanksgiving" (Psalm 95:2 KJV) and with joy: "You have made known to me the *path of life*; you will fill me with joy in your presence (Psalm 16:11, italics added).

Paul writes to the Thessalonian church that when Christ comes back, He will "be marveled at *among all those who have believed*" (2 Thessalonians 1:10, italics added). He also says that those who don't believe will be "shut out from the *presence* of the Lord" (v. 9, italics added). As a believer you find knowledge about your life's path as you mature your relationship *in His presence* daily. Because of what He gives you in that relationship (eternal life first, and then spiritual maturity and holiness), you enter His presence, not only with thanksgiving, but also with singing (Psalm 100:2). Praying unafraid, you "take refuge in the shelter of [His] wings" (Psalm 61:4), singing in His presence (Psalm 63:7). As your spiritual character matures, you remain in His presence daily, conforming to His standards (Psalm 140:13). His presence is everywhere; you can't move far enough to hide from Him (Psalm 139:7). He's always ready to talk with you.

Learn His Precepts

One important part of your relationship with Christ is a program of daily devotional reading from the Bible. This discipline is known as the *Lectro Divina*, or Divine Reading. Jesus said, "Seek first his kingdom [as explained in the Gospels] and his righteousness [as explained in His laws], and all these things [that we worry about] will be given to you as well" (Matthew 6:33). A focus on the divine, inspired Word of God is essential for growing your spiritual life. Carlisle Marnie said, "Why doesn't God speak to us as he did of old?" He held up his Bible. "Here He is! He does speak to us. Here's how He speaks: through His words here. Begin in His Word."

God's Word has changed great Christians in history. When Martin Luther read God's Word, he realized inequities existed in church leadership. He spoke about the truth he had read. When asked to recant from the things he'd said, he replied that he couldn't recant unless he was convinced by Scripture. ***Because one man had found truth in God's Word, the Protestant Reformation changed the world.***

In many Christians' daily devotion time, they memorize and pray Scriptures. If you want to be a growing, maturing Christian, follow this Christian's advice: "Don't read and forget. Read to memorize. Read to recall. Read to pray. Read to listen." You'll find certain passages come alive with the Spirit of God—His special word to you for that moment. Look for those words of revelation. Be open to His ideas, His precepts, His personal word for you at a given minute in time.

Experience His Power

Just as those who don't believe are "shut out from the presence of the Lord" (2 Thessalonians 1:9*a*), so will unbelievers be shut out "from the majesty of his power" (v. 9*b*). Maturing Christians acknowledge the real physical and spiritual power of our Sovereign God. The presence of God is awesome. "When mine enemies are turned back, they shall fall and perish *at thy presence*" (Psalm 9:3 KJV, italics added).

One of the most amazing powers of Christ is that He can cleanse your heart and make even the worst sinner pure: "Now unto him that is able to keep you from falling, and *to present you faultless before the presence of his glory*...to the only wise God our Saviour, be glory and majesty, dominion and power, both now and forever. Amen" (Jude 24–25 KJV, italics added).

In your own words, tell how you do the following:

Seek His presence:

Learn His precepts:

Experience His power:

Being, Not Doing

On one level or another, the story of the highway line painter at the beginning of this study is about us, since we often move further away from our spiritual bucket, our relationship with God. Bob Ferguson says, "We think life consists of 'doing' instead of 'being.' We emphasize what we do or accomplish as indicators that our lives are purposeful and meaningful." To be sure, what we "do" is an important indicator of our relationship with Jesus Christ—but only as an indicator, not as final proof of who we are. The good news of Jesus Christ is that *"being comes before doing."* Who you are in Christ, as you linger in His presence, determines what you do.

M&M: *Ministry and Missions Moment*

When I was a teenager, a mentor at church said to me, "Don't linger too long."

I replied, "There's no such thing as lingering too long with Jesus."

The mentor said, "I've found that I miss opportunities if I'm too contemplative. I never get up and serve. God wants me to have a balanced life: some soaking up the Savior, some spreading Him around to others." I've thought about those words many times. What are you doing to assure your maturing Christian life is balanced: some soaking up His presence, as Mary did; some spreading His precepts around, as a Martha?

Deeper Still: Mystery Revealed

Every aspect of Christian life can be difficult, sometimes even the usually joyous devotional times with our Lord. Jesus said, "The worries of this life, the deceitfulness of wealth and the desires for other things come in and choke the word" (Mark 4:19). When you discipline yourself to the routine of Bible reading, you may find dryness choking the divine Word. A mature Christian friend said, "We enjoy a daily life of devotion, but at times the Bible is a spoonful of sand, the sky is made of brass, and our prayers ricochet back to us." Here's a mystery of devotion: *Maturing Christians linger in the sand and brass.*

—— Study 17 ——
The Company You Keep

My mother told me often when I was a preteen, "If you want a friend, *be* a friend. Pick good friends and they'll be loyal." Her words are true. Godly friends are like mothers: they stand by you through adversity, encouraging you in good and bad times.

Dale Carnegie, in *How to Win Friends and Influence People*, explained a key concept: *Asking*. Carnegie wrote, called, and found ways to meet people. You also can ask others to be your friend. Speaking of making requests in prayer, God says, "Ask and it will be given to you; seek and you will find; knock and the door will be opened to you" (Matthew 7:7). James tells the first-century Church, "Ye *have* not because ye *ask* not" (James 4:2 KJV, italics added).

Carnegie went right to the top. He contacted famous people and found them lonely, eager to begin a friendship with him. He kept letters going as a genuine fan of those he admired. He was sincerely seeking a relationship with each of them, and they responded favorably. He learned many things sitting at the feet of famous men and women, and he also learned vicariously through their correspondence from distant places.

You do not have to settle for friendships with halfhearted people who have little backbone or character. Select friends whom you admire for their stalwart Christian character, their knowledge of God, and their enthusiasm for life.

Friends and Lovers Can Corrupt

The influence of spouses or close friends is incredible. It's easy for me to say, "Be careful when forming relationships or getting married," but forming alliances, friendships, or marriages is a delicate process as you bond with a loved one. Snow was a fairly good influence on my growth as a Christian. He was a good man, basically a moral man. He attended church on Sunday mornings and occasionally participated in other church activities. He gave good moral advice to me and our children, but he did not have an overflowing joy in his faith, and he had no desire to serve Jesus in a sacrificial way.

One night Snow expressed sadness over his halfhearted service to God. When I asked what kept him from making Jesus not only his Savior but also his Lord, he confessed a fantasy of immorality with a certain woman that kept him from giving his whole heart to the Lord. He explained that if that beautiful woman flirted with him, he feared he couldn't say no. To be honest, I had to bite my cheeks to keep from laughing. Though he was a wonderful person, I could never see this woman making such a proposition to him. His fantasy was totally unrealistic: this beautiful woman had a good reputation and was happily married. I was sure she would never have flirted with him. Shortly thereafter, Snow recognized the immorality of his secret fantasy and gave his whole heart to God. Once he'd confessed his fantasy to me, it began to diminish. Before long, he far surpassed me in his dedication to Christ and his courage to witness.

Several years ago, while sharing with a large church in Ohio, for some reason I felt led to tell the group about my husband (then deceased) and his confession 12 years before. After I told the story of my husband's conversion from a lukewarm Christian clinging to an immoral fantasy to a courageous witness, a woman came up confessing a similar sin. Harboring her secret, she was on the brink of beginning an illicit relationship with someone else's husband.

I seldom speak at a women's conference now without meeting at least one woman who says sheepishly, "I live with another woman's husband," or "I'm sleeping with my boyfriend, but I don't think that keeps me from being a Christian; do you?" I know sexual sins—especially elusive fantasies of lust—are a prevalent problem, because they seem harmless, yet they lead to the next step: an illicit relationship. If you are a Christian who has slipped back into a carnal life, ask God to help you remain pure every day.

I've also prayed for many men whose wives have been devastated because their husbands fell in love with other women. Sometimes these men have later come repentantly to their wives, saying, "I don't understand it. What happened to me? My behavior for the past year is not like me. I'm sorry." Satan offers physical attraction as one of his strongest weapons for destroying Christians. Maturing Christians learn to become alert to such dangers. If you want to be a stronger Christian, examine now the secret sins of your heart, look at them honestly, and ask God to help you cleanse every dark spot.

Deeper Still

Refuse the Refuse in Your Life

You know what your areas of temptation are. Recognize the people who are not beneficial to your moral development and cut ties with them. God says, "If your eye causes you to sin, pluck it out. It is better for you to enter the kingdom of God with one eye than to have two eyes and be thrown into hell" (Mark 9:47). You can refuse the refuse (trash, garbage) in your own life. If you have friends who lead you into temptation, you have the wrong friends. If you have friends who hang around the fringes of drugs, alcohol, and sexual immorality, muster up your courage and keep your distance. Whatever it is—a person or an activity—that keeps you from being the most godly Christian you can be, pluck it out of your life. Throw it away. Refuse to accept it in your life again. Mind the company you keep. (Read also study 22, "Relaying Wisdom.")

Which of the following are you willing to do to keep yourself in good company rather than in ungodly company?

❑ Join a Bible-believing, evangelical church.
❑ Join mission societies or read information about godly organizations.
❑ Go on a mission trip.
❑ Find Christian friends in your neighborhood.
❑ Seek Christian friends at work.
❑ Invite Christians to join you in a crafting group, bowling league, ball team, golf tournament, or other form of recreation.
❑ Pray, staying close to Jesus.

Write the initials of someone you might befriend: a neighbor, distant relative, or spiritually younger person you may guide, teach, counsel, encourage, or serve in some way: _____

List below several talents, skills, or spiritual gifts you might teach or share:

Set a possible time and date you'll approach the person to offer your friendship in a Christian mentoring relationship.

Seek the Best; Seek the Worst

In the preceding paragraphs, we discussed seeking only the best people for friends. However, sometimes God may call you to minister to people involved in drugs, alcohol, or sexual immorality. If God calls you to minister to someone with such needs, walk wisely, keep your life in balance, and seek wisdom from a strong Christian confidante when accepting His call. Also, do not attempt to minister in an area where you know you are vulnerable, like going with an alcoholic friend to a party where there will be alcohol if that has been something you yourself have battled. *Ask a prayer triplet (three spiritually mature people) to pray for you as you represent godliness and enter an ungodly place or situation.* Pray for your own personal purity and for God's shield of protection around you. "He is my loving God and my fortress, my stronghold and my deliverer, my shield, in whom I take refuge" (Psalm 144:2).

M&M: *Ministry and Missions Moment*

Jesus is "able to do immeasurably more than all we ask or imagine, according to his power that is at work within us, to him be glory in the church and in Christ Jesus throughout all generations, for ever and ever! Amen" (Ephesians 3:20–21). This month set aside time to *pray about all the generations you may touch with the gospel.* Act on the ministries for which God has given you passion among "the company you keep."

Deeper Still: Mystery Revealed

Here's a true mystery that is unbelievable until you see it clearly: *Trash often looks good.* Satan packages it attractively. Ask God to peruse your heart today, showing you *refuse you need to refuse*! Pray for clear vision and courage to take out the trash.

—— Study 18 ——
Stepping Out

A contemplative life always leads to an outer focus. D. A. Ousley says, "Scripture provides an 'Other-centeredness' to cure the self-centeredness that is ours from the Fall." In *Friend to Friend*, this concept is called "undering" and "othering" (pp. 8–9, 51–53). We need an *other-centeredness*, a life filled with Christian actions.

Hot-Wired Christians

Retired missionary Herbert Neely says these three characteristics identify a life of lasting Christian actions:

1. They begin from God; that is, being in His will.
2. They have a life aglow with the Holy Spirit.
3. They bring glory to God.

God is the generator, or power source, for your life. You're the hot wire, running from Him to the world. In His will, filled with His power, you illuminate the world. Your thanksgiving and praises are the neutral wire that returns to the generator. The electrical circuit will not work unless the neutral wire keeps the connection going. As in the life of David, maturing Christians need to be in constant connection to their Lord.

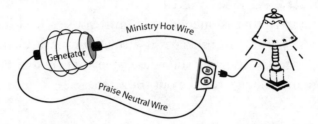

On this generator chart, write your name where you're most comfortable, absorbing power inside the generator, moving out as the hot wire in the world, at the point of contact illuminating the world, or returning the connection as a neutral wire.

List things you'll do in each place, as God directs you.

Bubble Christians

One key concept for being God's hot wire to change the world is *other*. You are born with the concept of *self*, but one of the human stages indicating normal child maturation is the concept of otherness. When left with other caregivers, children initially miss their parents, but begin missing them less after a while and start interacting with other people, especially children. How aware are you of the needs of others? Some Christians have a natural outer focus; others, a natural inner focus. Some are people oriented; others are task oriented. Whatever our personalities, as maturing Christians, we must step outside our comfort zones and care about others as Jesus does.

An unhealthy Christian trend has become popular with twenty-first-century Americans. They stay in Christian circles. They shop at Christian clubs, use Christian telephone service, homeschool their children, listen only to Christian radio, and never step outside their protective bubble. Instead of being an influence on an ungodly world, they bury their heads in the sand, never ever knowing how the world is changing. They may be absorbing power in the generator, but they don't have a healthy system of flowing out like hot wires to the world.

A fellow worker, a Christian, asked a neighbor to go with us to a nursing home. She said, "I'd never do that. I don't want my children to see or smell places like that." The residents of that facility missed the joy of children bringing them bananas, and the children missed an opportunity to change the world. It's sad to know those children's hearts will never be exposed to the tug for missions and benevolence, which are close to God's heart. They may grow up as bubble Christians, locked behind a protective shield, never experiencing the joy of "othering": caring for others and sharing the miracle of a Christ-centered heart.

"Other" People Out There

As we isolate ourselves, we forget that "other" people are "out there." We speak of *us* and *them*. Prejudice grows rampantly. Jesus, our perfect example of relating to the world, taught us to think about others. As He walked His paths, He stopped and compassionately loved people, whatever their station in life. He had a meal in Zaccheus's home, though he was a short, apparently dishonest tax collector (Luke 19:2–10). Jesus became the friend of publicans, known for their haughtiness (Matthew 5:46). He asked Matthew, probably a hated tax collector, to become one of His twelve disciples (Matthew 9:9–12). He welcomed the Roman centurion, even though this military man may have killed or harassed many people. He spoke to prostitutes and immoral women and defended them (Luke 7:31–50; John 4:1–42; 8:1–11). If lines of moral behavior had been drawn in the sand by the Jews, Jesus stepped over them to minister to those on the other side! He accepted all humanity, disbarring traditional prejudices. (We'll discuss more about prejudice in study 28.)

Draw a picture (or a stick figure) of each of these people, as you think the world would view them today. By each name, list their characteristics as you imagine them.

Zaccheus

Publicans

Matthew

The Centurion

Prostitutes

Have you ever been prejudiced against any one of these types? Explain:

How can you cross barriers today?

A Maturing Christian Witnesses

One major characteristic of a mature Christian is a passion for witnessing. In her book *Spiritual Life Development*, Mildred McMurry said, "If you have no desire to share Jesus, then your Christianity is very shallow." Go deeper. Share from an overflow. Herschel Hobbs said, "Under all circumstances we can witness for Christ."

Reaching Out to Untouchables

A maturing Christian has the capability and inclination to reach out to those the world considers "untouchables."

Tony Campolo tells the story of being hungry in a strange town and going into a diner in the early morning hours. In a few minutes he realized the group of women who'd entered were prostitutes, getting off for the evening. He heard one of them, "Agnes," say her thirty-ninth birthday was the next day. Sarcastically others made fun of her, saying not to expect them to give her a party. She said she knew they wouldn't give her one, since no one else had in her lifetime.

After they left, Campolo learned from the restaurant manager that the group came in every night about the same time. The next evening, after he'd spoken at a Christian conference, he returned. With the manager's permission, Campolo decorated the diner for a birthday party, complete with gifts and a birthday cake. When the women came in, imagine the surprise of the "birthday girl" when she saw the decorations. All the women seemed to enjoy it. Afterward, she asked, "What kind of church do you go to?"

He replied, "The kind that has a party for a prostitute."

"No, you don't," she said. "Because if they did, I'd be there."

M&M: *Ministry and Missions Moment*

I sounds easy when someone says, "Step out in God," but as a maturing Christian, you know that's a fallacy. It costs to step out in faith. *Sharing Jesus may cost you everything you own.* My husband worked for years before he decided to witness in his workplace. When he did, his worst fears came true. One of his best friends, a marginal Christian, stopped speaking to him, even avoiding him in social settings. (After months of turning a cold-shoulder, this friend experienced a crisis and called on us for help, rededicating his life to God.) Ask God to help you step out boldly in full armor

(Ephesians 6:10–18), exposing your Christianity to all your circles of influence. Step over barriers, regardless of the cost.

Deeper Still: Mystery Revealed

Paul says, "Do not deceive yourselves. If any one of you thinks he is wise by the standards of this age, he should become a 'fool' so that he may become wise. For the wisdom of this world is foolishness in God's sight" (1 Corinthians 3:18–19). Here's the mystery: *to become wise, mature Christians become fools in the eyes of the world.* Forget the world; step out of the physical world and into the Spirit.

—— Study 19 ——

Beginning at Home

One of my Sunday School Bible study members, "Madison," came up after a lesson on Christian maturity. "If I could just get 'James' to be a better husband, I could be a better wife and mother. He irritates me, has no idea how to love us, and won't set a good example before our children."

"What are you doing to help him?" I asked.

"I tell him every day what he ought to be doing: taking out the trash, helping with the dishes, driving the children to school, being unselfish.... I've worked on him since the day we got married, but all my trying has not changed him a bit. Once he changes, we can have a good Christian home. Until then, I'm hopeless." As we talked, she blamed James for her own bad attitude. She said they quarreled every day, and each time it was his fault. He made her explode constantly. It was evident Madison was the quarreling one; James sat quietly, refusing to talk after her tongue-lashings.

The Fragility of the Home

John Charles Ryle said, "Readiness to quarrel is not the mark of holiness." In his book *Holiness*, he says immense harm is done to the cause of Christ "if we say we've received a blessing or have seen the light or found a higher life *and yet are not kinder at home*" (italics added). Those who want to be more mature in their Christian walk need to take a close look at the way they relate to their families. The greatest tool for evangelism is the Christian home. More people become Christians through it than any other way, yet *the home is a fragile place.*

The Deep Love of the Mature Christian

God's plan is that families celebrate every day together. Does that sound like your family? Probably not. *It's unrealistic to think that every day will be a holiday* when your spouse is not perfect, your children are rebelling, and sibling rivalry grows out of sight. Yet we can be an influence on all our family and say with Joshua, "As for me and my house, we will serve the LORD" (Joshua 24:15 KJV). The Bible is filled with examples of good homes, as well as bad, so we can see the difference. We can learn the following principles from God's Word.

Mature Christians Deeply Love Their Spouses

Genesis begins by establishing the human home, which became the world's first institution, with two people: Adam and Eve. The best thing a husband and wife can do for their children is to love each other—physically, mentally, socially, and spiritually. *After the honeymoon period, your marital love moves from the physical level to deeper levels of spiritual love:* a tenderness and unselfishness akin to that of God, who loves you unconditionally. One of the hardest relationships is that between spouses because the relationship is the most intimate on earth. Can you say, as Christ did about His

bride, the Church, that you love your husband unconditionally—
that you will love him without self-interest? (Read Ephesians
5:25.) Your unselfish words and actions reflect your Christian
maturity.

**If you are married, take a long look at your husband today. Write
all the things you like about him.**

Write the things you dislike about your husband.

Write the things you think your husband likes about you.

Write the things you think your husband dislikes about you.

**Write the things you think Christ likes about you, as you relate
to your husband.**

**Write the things you think Christ dislikes about you, as you
relate to your husband.**

Pray now for the ability and willingness to change to become more Christlike in your relationship with your husband.

Mature Christians Deeply Love Their Children

One mark of mature Christians is their respect for children, whether they are yours or someone else's. As they grow from infancy into maturity in your home, family, or neighborhood, they are molded into buds of the people they are going to be in the future, whether Christian or unbeliever. The principles you share with children are never wasted. The way you treat children is an indication of your Christian love.

From experience, I know rearing children is the hardest job in the world. As the old saying goes, "Children are arrows; parents are the bow." You must be stretched and pulled taut, bent out of shape before you're able to launch them into adulthood. However, as the adult, you are the mature leader. Maturing Christians make good parents, are able to show love out of an overflow of Christ's love in them, administer discipline in love, and, above all, forgive.

Mature Christians Deeply Love Parents and Grandparents

In one of his letters, Paul refers to a mature Christian family: Eunice, Lois, and Timothy. Paul and other Christians in the first century recognized them as examples. Paul writes to Timothy, his co-worker and fellow minister in the gospel, "I thank God, whom I serve...as night and day I constantly remember you in my prayers.... I have been reminded of your sincere faith, which first lived in your grandmother Lois and in your mother Eunice and, I am persuaded, now lives in you also" (2 Timothy 1:3, 5). We know little about this family, but we can assume that Timothy showed deep love for his mother Eunice and his grandmother Lois by serving Christ, following their spiritual tradition.

If you have children or grandchildren, consider ways you can encourage them to continue their spiritual growth. My grandfather said many times to my cousins: "I have asked God to give me one grandchild who is a preacher." His prayer was answered, with two ordained ministers and many others who are full-time or part-time church or denominational staff. They've carried on the tradition of showing love to each other and to their parents and grandparents.

Mature Christians Deeply Love Their Siblings

In *Transformed*, Stuart Calvert said, "To speak to a brother about the Lord often takes more courage and faith than to speak to a stranger." Sibling rivalry extends into adulthood and, if the siblings are immature, festers into old age. What can you do for your siblings today?

The greatest example of immaturity arises when parents die. As a maturing Christian, make sure that you plan ahead for times of bereavement. Start now building a foundation of love and trust with your siblings.

Circle the following phrases that show some possibilities of building relationships with your siblings:

A visit   A phone call

A note of apology   A long talk

Dinner and/or a movie   A valentine expressing your love

A family reunion   An extravagant gift

Free babysitting   Sharing...with no strings attached

Mature Christians Deeply Love Their In-Laws

During a women's retreat at Bambi Lake Conference Center, Roscommon, Michigan, Anne Kinzer told me this story: "Sara" had reluctantly joined a small group after a worship service. She sat with defensive body language: tight-lipped, arms crossed, in a stiff position. When asked to share, Sara said, "On the way up to Bambi Lake, I asked the women in our van to pray for me to have a better relationship with my mother-in-law. I've tried, but I just can't like that woman."

She paused. "Then tonight in this worship session, when the speaker led us in the Bible study about Ruth and Naomi, she said, 'God is calling you now to a deep Spirit-led relationship with your mother-in-law. You need to see to it that your mother-in-law *knows* you love her—and you *need* to love her—*sincerely.*'"

The next day the small group met again and Sara said, "I'm not saying this retreat had anything to do with this, but I've decided to love my mother-in-law. I think I can...really love her."

Ruth loved her mother-in-law, Naomi. She left her own family to follow in Naomi's tradition, and she grew in maturity at Naomi's instruction (Ruth 1–4). She set the example of unselfish *in-law love*. In the last few years, I have felt God calling me to be an influencer of young women who do not have the adoring relationship Ruth had with her mother-in-law.

In-Law Love Scale

If your mother-in-law (or son-in-law, daughter-in-law, etc.) makes the following remarks, how will you react? Select a, b, or c for the following five questions:

1. May I go into your kitchen and wash that sinkful of dirty dishes?
   a. Don't you dare touch my kitchen, you old bat! You're insulting me.
   b. Thanks, but I'll get to it later. I've just been busy.
   c. Oh, I'm so grateful for your kind offer. Yes! You're the greatest!

2. I brought a lasagna casserole. I know how my son loves it, and he never gets that from you.
   a. I serve him what he deserves, as badly as he treats me, the ungrateful cad!
   b. I love your lasagna, too! What a wonderful gift!
   c. Thanks, but no thanks. I have a good lasagna from the Italian restaurant around the corner.

3. What is that smell? Have you been cooking again, or is your sewer backed up?
   a. You have a sensitive nose. And a snoopy one, too…always prying, always hurting me.
   b. I love your sense of humor! Let's investigate. Thank you for helping me diagnose it.
   c. Why don't you go home, if you don't like the way my home smells?

4. I don't understand why you don't take the children to church every Sunday.
   a. And I don't understand why you think it's any of your business!
   b. We've not missed a Sunday this year until last week. How could you say such a thing?
   c. I've been really tired lately. As kind as you are, if you noticed it, I need to look at my life to see if it's a physical or a spiritual problem. I probably need to make some changes. Maybe you could help me.

5. The children are outgrowing their clothes. Do you need me to make some play outfits for them?
   a. They'd love to have something their sweet grandmother made for them! Thanks.

b. Are you kidding? I don't want them dressed in ugly clothes like the horrors you wear.

c. No! (silence)

If you chose 1-c, 2-b, 3-b, 4-c, and 5-a, you are an ideal in-law love expert. Charity begins at home. Without being insincere, think of kind loving words with which you can address your in-laws. Abide in stage 6 of moral development: Do unto others as you would have them do unto you.

Compliment and build the confidence of your in-laws whenever possible. Think of other strategies for positively influencing them:

Mature Christians Deeply Love Extended Family

Like Leah and Rachel; Hagar and Sarah; Rebekah, Jacob, and Esau, you may have blended families or special problems with your extended family. Ask God to give you overwhelming love for all connected to your family. One of the closest members of my family is my aunt Alice, who was 16 when my mother, my brother, and I lived with Alice and my grandparents during my father's military service. She became my constant companion, inviting Jim and me to movies at a local theater where she worked, taking us swimming, and asking our advice on her outfits for special occasions. We thought she was the most beautiful young woman in the world! She has continued to be beautiful as she has mentored me, taken care of my children, brought food in times of sickness, and taught me about spiritual maturity.

You can be the catalyst for your extended family—aunts, uncles, cousins, divorced/estranged/extended/distant family members— helping each one feel encouraged and loved, regardless of problems in the past.

Mature Christians Deeply Love Over-the-Fence Friends

When I was 38, I had major surgery. For the first time in my life, I was immobile, not able to get out, ride around town, or run errands. I sat most of the day embroidering or watching television, eager to have some task I could do. My next-door neighbor, Linda Sparks, came several times, bringing a macaroni-and-cheese casserole each time. She'll never know how much that meant to me! Linda, with a full-time job, took time—an hour or two—to make the casserole from scratch, and her sacrifice was greatly appreciated, not only by me, but by my hungry husband and children. Neighbors can be like family. Reach out to them as sisters and brothers.

M&M: *Ministry and Missions Moment*

Just for today, forget your usual ministry to outsiders (unless it would be breaking a commitment to do so). Spend a day of love dedicated to your family. Look around you and pray that God will show you ways to give unselfishly. Ask Him to take away family resentment in your heart and fill you with overflowing love. May God's richest blessings flow to and through you as you express your heart to your family. Remember, charity begins at home.

Deeper Still: *Mystery Revealed*

John Charles Ryle said that *after a church meeting, each of us should be "more holy, meek, unselfish, kind, good-tempered, self-denying, and Christlike at home."* He explains what he means: growing Christians are (1) content with their position in life; (2) free from restless cravings; (3) able to enjoy a quiet Sunday without noise, heat, and excitement; and (4) growing in charity toward those who do not agree with them. Think about each of these characteristics of mature Christians. Ask God to make your heart and your actions more Christlike at home.

—— Study 20 ——
Reaching the Top: A Paradox

Saying "We're marching to Zion," or "we're walking on the upward way" appeals to our sense of drama and inspiration, but the truth is that as God increases in importance, we diminish. We don't go upward, we go downward and deeper. A maturing Christian is *willing and able* to take the last place, the lowest rung on the ladder, in order to love God for God's sake.

Milestones Along the Way

God teaches us every day. As we live longer, we experience more and more wisdom and truth. Yet as maturing Christians, we don't have a sense of being "at the top." You may know several famous people who are at the top (or at least you've seen them on television); they've achieved greatness in one arena or another. They talk about their money, their awards, and their possessions. On the contrary, to reach the top of Christian maturity, you need to strive to get to the bottom. The top is at the bottom.

What do you consider the rewards of people at the top?

Why is reaching the top a paradox?

Giving Away Toys: A Milestone

Sue Carver tells this story about Elizabeth Reaves ("Miss Libby"), Sue's childhood Sunday School teacher, now deceased: "I appreciate the investment Miss Libby made in my life during those impressionable years. One truth of God's character I learned from her guidance happened one Christmas. She asked us to give up some of our nice toys (not discards) to provide presents for others. When I later saw the toys—some I had enjoyed, cherished, and protected—lying broken and abandoned in the yard of the new owners, I was angry. Why would the new owners not appreciate my sacrifice? Many years later, still mad, I got the 'aha' of that experience.

"Imagine how God must feel about our response to His gift of His Son to us. Through Jesus Christ, we are given permission to spend every minute of every component of our life forever in the presence and wisdom of Almighty God. We discount His sacrifice when we ignore, discard, or show casual and infrequent interest in His gift. To avoid access to Jesus means we don't understand the value of the gift. *Our unnecessary spiritual poverty is the source of God's grief.* Thank you, Miss Libby, for letting me see how you appreciated God's gift in your everyday events."

Giving Away Control: A Milestone

In another letter, Sue also comments on what she learned about giving gifts to the poor: "*Poor* is not a term limited to people with no money. The truly poor are those without a fully activated 'follower-ship' for Christ, regardless of their financial condition. Christ said give ALL our wealth to the poor. No other goals are an acceptable substitute. The command God gives is *not* followed by a promise to replenish what is given. Once all is given, it is gone.

I no longer control how or *if* the wealth will ever benefit me. In the giving, I have chosen for others to have more than I, to benefit from what I once owned. Isn't that the essence of what Christ has done for us? He gave all to the poor (us).

"Until we see our state of emptiness, helplessness, and brokenness as a destitute condition, we do not comprehend what complete dependence on God means. We are spiritual paupers who have experienced the grace of a generous God."

Seeing Through the Veil: A Milestone

If you're a maturing Christian, you've learned the following:

❦ **The more you know, the more you realize you don't know.** And we, who with unveiled faces all reflect the Lord's glory, are being transformed into his likeness" (2 Corinthians 3:18). The more mature we become, the more transparent becomes the veil separating us from eternal truth. I call this the veil of mortality, because it is our mortality, our fleshly humanness, which clouds our view of spiritual things. It's ironic that once we're able to glimpse eternal truth, we see how far away from holiness we actually are. The closer to Jesus we become, the more painfully aware we are of our shortcomings.

You're able to see this kind of eternal Truth because Jesus said, "I am the way and the *truth* and the life. No one comes to the Father except *through* me" (John 14:6, italics added). You're able to relate to Truth because Truth is a person: the Person of Jesus. The more you're absorbed into the heart of Christ, the more you can see with your spiritual eyes—with *His* eyes. In Hebrews 10:16, He says, "I will put my laws in their hearts, and I will write them on their minds"—a totally *inner* process!

As the veil becomes transparent, and you get glimpses of Truth, you realize that Jesus *is* the veil. His Word says, "We have confidence to enter the Most Holy Place by the blood of Jesus, by a new and living way opened for us through the curtain, that is, his body" (Hebrews 10:19–20). You are able to see God without the Veil of Mortality separating you from heaven because Jesus helps you enter through the curtain, that is, His body. His body is the way through which you learn Truth and become a mature Christian. Because He died for you, giving His body as a sacrifice, you have access to heaven and eternal life.

❧ **You've learned that the suffering you once hated has led you to obedience.** Jesus is the perfect example of suffering. "During the days of Jesus's life on earth, he offered up prayers and petitions with loud cries and tears.... Although he was a son, he learned obedience through suffering" (Hebrews 5:7–8). Like Him, you've become submissive as you learn obedience through your own suffering, especially when you suffered for the cause of Christ. Because of your love for Him, you're willing to suffer for the joy of the race as well as the reward at the end—eternal life in the presence of Jesus. (This topic will be discussed in detail in study 26.)

❧ **You've grown from immaturity** (literally meaning "dull of hearing") through distractions and now have sensitive ears, able to hear and experience Truth. Through practice, your senses have become trained to discern good and evil; with a certain "wariness of the Holy Spirit," you can sense goodness and evil in others. You've realized that spiritual wisdom is more valuable than formerly desired wisdom acquired in the world. You're able to recognize evil, which intensifies in opposition to you as you mature spiritually. The closer you grow to God, the more intensely you feel the attacks of Satan and the need for spiritual-warfare praying. (On the prayer triangle on page 62, trace the path of evil on the right as your spiritual maturity deepens as indicated on the left.)

❦ **You've become a teacher.** A mature Christian couple once said, "We have become teachers—but we never thought we'd make it." As we saw in study 1, Christians move from infancy and "milk" to adulthood and "meat." Time in Christ's presence mellows us as it matures us; as we become more contemplative, we realize we have matured enough to become teachers, not just learners. At the same time, we realize we'll always be learners, and the maturation process on earth never ends.

❦ **You're not entangled by external Christian rituals** because you know spiritual maturity does not come from them. They are not a means to spiritual maturity, but are by-products of spiritual maturity. We don't realize these are by-products until we, in retrospect, realize life is more than what we see on earth. We can see glimpses of eternity—*God signs*—through the veil.

Marking Milestones

As you look back, marking milestones on your spiritual journey, look for the *God signs* along the path.

Have you given up control of something valuable in your life lately? If so, explain:

How has God called you to give up control?

List the milestones of your journey toward spiritual maturity:

When is your veil of mortality (times when you can't see spiritual truth) the thickest? Explain.

A Stone for Your Anchor

For several years, I carried a small stone in my pocket as a memento of times God had allowed me to witness. (I'd studied the way God's people used stones as altars to honor Him, remembering miracles He'd performed.) As the stone became heavier, God reminded me that it was His heavy anchor to keep me, a naturally sanguine personality, from soaring too high. Even without the stone, I'm reminded nearly every day that Jesus is our Rock, our anchor. "We have this hope as an anchor for the soul, firm and secure. It enters the inner sanctuary behind the curtain, where Jesus, who went before us, has entered on our behalf" (Hebrews 6:19–20). Just as Old Testament people did, I used my stone as an altar of praise to the Almighty, whose presence also had carried me through the veil or curtain. God has blessed you and me far more than we deserve. Give Him the praise for what He has done for you and then praise *Him* for what *you* have done for Him. It is only through Him that you are able to serve the Living God!

The Old Testament is full of incidents of placing stones to mark renewal. At Bethel, Jacob dreamed of a ladder to heaven. At the top, God Himself spoke a promise of blessing to Jacob: "All peoples on earth will be blessed through you and your offspring.... I will not leave you" (Genesis 28:14–15). The next morning, Jacob made a large pillow stone into an altar. Years later, Jacob made a covenant with his father-in-law, Laban, by piling stones at Mizpah for an altar "as a witness" and as a border between their lands (Genesis 31:44–49). When crossing the Jordan into the Promised Land, the Israelites took stones from the middle of the river, made the altar permanent with plaster, and wrote His Law on it so their descendants would know what God had done there (Deuteronomy 27:1–3; Joshua 4).

The Bible speaks of Christ as the Cornerstone of the Church (Isaiah 28:16; Ephesians 2:20–22; 1 Peter 2:6). He is the base, or foundation of our Christian maturity. As we are grounded—on the Cornerstone of our church structure, *on Him*—we can see ourselves in the total picture, with all Christians working together as a team, without any stars or excess pride, but all pulling together as one body. In his letter to the church at Colosse, Paul says "God has chosen to make known among the Gentiles the glorious riches of this mystery, which is Christ in you, the hope of glory" (Colossians 1:27). As mentioned earlier, He also encourages you to be *sure* you know. As a maturing Christian, you know the mystery of *"Christ in you, the hope of glory."* You rest at the bottom, without pride, on the Stone, who is your anchor. Remember, the further you go on the Christian journey, the deeper you move toward the bottom, the Rock of your salvation.

M&M: *Ministry and Missions Moment*

Paul tells new Christians at Corinth, to whom he had witnessed earlier, "By the grace God has given me, I laid a foundation as an expert builder, and someone else is building on it.... No one can lay any foundation other than the one already laid, which is Jesus Christ" (1 Corinthians 3:10–11). If we build on others' stones, then we are edifying the Church. This month, be alert to the *God signs* in your life. Where is God working around you? Jump into that circle, and get busy. Find a place of service in a solid Christian ministry as you build on the Cornerstone of faith, Jesus Christ, and the foundation others have laid. Mature your faith there.

Deeper Still: *Mystery Revealed*

Maturing Christians focus on *the deep* to achieve *the upward*. Paul says, "Listen, I tell you a mystery. We…will all be changed—in a flash, in the twinkling of an eye, at the last trumpet. For the trumpet will sound, the dead will be raised imperishable" (1 Corinthians 15:52). Meditate today on this mysterious dichotomy: *The deeper you dive, the higher you'll soar.* Think of ways you can go deeper into God's Word and His Spirit, anticipating the imperishable life you'll have in heaven.

Unit 5

———————— • ————————

REACHING OUT TO THE ENDS OF THE EARTH

And then, surprised, O God! I'm not ashamed. I tell the world.
I spill the words; I cross the street; I go, I run, I fly!

And underneath Your mighty wings I pray, Lord, hold me up.
I yield to You, as You pull deeper still, but higher, God.

I trust; I lean; I hide in You. My confidence is sure.
I pass the love to others, innocent lambs, beloved.

Your work in hearts magnificent: no falling, fainting now,
But soaring with a wonder, awesome thunder, lightning-fire!

Study 21

Open to Opportunities

A California pastor told me this story: A stamp collector sold his stamps at auction. A certain stamp was extremely rare: one of only two in the world. The bidding went up and up, and the stamp was finally sold for $168,000! Even the seller was astounded, not to mention customers who bid on the stamp earlier. The bidding over, they watched as the buyer came up to claim his stamp, which he took out of the glassine sleeve and ripped into several pieces, rendering it worthless.

"Why on earth did you do that?" gasped the auctioneer.

"I own the other one like it," said the buyer.

He had been watching for years, looking for a chance to buy the other stamp like the one he had, to skyrocket the price for the final one left in the world. He greedily checked until finally he had the opportunity to pounce on the opportunity to triple his money. In the eyes of the world, he was a winner. Some might consider him an *opportunist*, who exploited or took advantage of others.

Though people admired him as a shrewd collector of treasures, you don't expect that kind of worldly wise admiration as a maturing Christian; rather you look for God's approval as you seek treasures much more valuable than a thousand-dollar stamp. Jesus said, "Store up for yourselves treasures in heaven, where moth and rust do not destroy, and where thieves do not break in and steal. For where your treasure is, there your heart will be also" (Matthew 6:20–21). You're looking for God's treasures, and your heart is open to opportunities to minister in His name.

As a Christian, do you approve of what the new buyer of the stamp did?

What kind of opportunities do you have to store up treasure?

Instead of doubling your money, what kind of things can you double?

Chosen in Ministry

Sometimes God chooses unlikely people to be His ministers. In the early history of the 12 children of Jacob (Israel), the descendants of Levi had not been favored because of Levi's violent temper and behavior (Genesis 49:5–7), but when God chose to bring the mistreated Israelites out of Egypt, He chose a Levite to be their leader. He gave Moses and his brother Aaron, both Levites, places of honor. God chose them as spiritual leaders, a tradition continuing for hundreds of years. Even when they settled in the Promised Land, they didn't have to work the land for a living as other tribes did. The other tribes gave ten percent of their wealth to the Levites, who served in the tabernacle and later in the Jewish temple in Jerusalem. Their lives are a testimony to the forgiveness of God. *As a display of His glory, He chooses a wrecked life and changes the worst among us into the best among us.* If God calls you to give your life as a minister of the gospel, do not begin with a defeatist attitude. He calls whom He wants to call. As you saw in study 13, false humility can prevent you from acting in faith, as God calls you. Through the eyes of faith, think now of all the opportunities available.

Besides being a pastor or serving as church staff, list other ministry opportunities as possibilities:

What is your area of secular passion? List below those things you enjoy doing that could be used in a special ministry:

If money or time were no object, what would you do for God?

Ask God to show you if He wants you to be a career minister or a volunteer for Him. Spend time now in prayer, seeking His will as you mature in your Christian life.

Hopscotch Squares

However and wherever God calls you to serve, you will begin at home, as discussed in study 19. Think of home as the first hopscotch square, a place where you feel comfortable, but where you can establish a base from which to move out. Starting with *square one*, move from square to square, reaching further outward.

❧ **Square One Ministry: Do an assessment of your home.** Which opportunities do you have inside your home? Go through your house, room by room, in an attitude of prayer, asking God to stop you at places that are in His will. For instance, if He stops you at your kitchen range, He may have opportunities for you to bless others through your favorite recipe: take a "religious casserole" to a bereaved family, provide an order-in meal accompanied by your homemade pie for an aunt who needs a boost, or celebrate an "unbirthday party" with your family's favorite food. Even if you think you don't have the spiritual gift of hospitality, God can help you find a square one ministry at home. Another stop may be before the Bible, where God calls you to teach verses to your children and grandchildren, or by an old chair where you used to pray.

Which of the following is God leading you to do? Pray over each item below, circling the ones God shows you are in your areas of opportunity for ministry:

Storytelling

Providing transportation

Teaching

Playing a musical instrument

Playing sports

Drawing/painting

Sewing/quilting

Bookkeeping/budget management

Other (Be specific.):

Cooking

Leading in craft activities

Singing

Working with children

Working with teens

Working with adults

Gardening/flower arranging

What will you do about your diagnosis above? Write one opportunity you have to use your skills or talents to share Christ's love:

❦ **Square Two Ministry: Do an assessment of your neighborhood.** God's Word points to many areas of community service. For example, read Matthew 25:35–40.

"I was hungry and you gave me something to eat, I was thirsty and you gave me something to drink" (v. 35). Look at each of these areas. Do you know of an area near you with hungry people? Do all of them have pure water handy? (You may be surprised how many people don't have pure running water in their houses.)

"I was a stranger and you invited me in" (v. 35). How many internationals live within ten miles of your home? Again, you may be surprised at the number. If you eat at any Asian or Mexican restaurants, you'll find people needing English lessons and cultural life skills.

"I needed clothes and you clothed me" (v. 36). Most schools have children who need warm coats or underwear. School nurses and educators can point out needs of neglected children, and you can plug into programs helping these innocent, suffering ones.

"I was sick and you looked after me" (v. 36) In a similar way, hospitals need ministries to the sick and dying, especially to children. Often mothers of chronically or terminally ill children need to work to keep their insurance, and the vicious cycle prevents a parental presence with the child. Check out the lonely ones, young and old, in your local hospitals, nursing homes, and other care facilities. Besides one-on-one care, you can also contribute to research and preventative measures, perhaps through your church.

"I was in prison and you came to visit me" (v. 36). If you've never known inmates in jail or prison, you don't know their family's heartache. Families need you to minister to them, to serve as lay counselors, to offer parental guidance, to share the Bible, to donate special foods, and to teach literacy. Lonely people behind bars need a personal touch. Working through prison chaplains, you can

accomplish many things in restorative justice. You'll find ideas for various community ministries at www.projecthelp.com.

Jesus says, *"I tell you the truth, whatever you did for one of the least of these brothers of mine, you did for me"* (v. 40).

❧ **Square Three Ministry: Do an assessment of your church.** Look in your church bulletin for opportunities to use the gifts God has given you to bless others. Visit your pastor or staff ministry/ missions leader to find out needs you may meet. You may volunteer to help with records or answer the phone in the office, give furniture or clothes to your crisis centers, or just be on call as a need arises. If you have no church home, visit the one nearest you and find out about what opportunities they have for someone with your skills, talents, and spiritual gifts. If you're an active church member, you probably have served in some sort of position in your local church or in a church organization as God has led you. Perhaps you work full time in a church or ministry, or you are thinking about doing so.

The Bible portrays a rich heritage of church ministers. Read 1 Chronicles 26:12–24. "These divisions…had duties for ministering in the temple of the LORD, just as their relatives had" (v. 12). Scriptures mention Zechariah as a wise counselor at the North Gate of the temple (v. 14). The sons of Obed-Edom took care of the storehouse, or the treasury; and Shubael, a direct descendant of Moses, was the officer in charge (vv. 15, 24). Other Levites were assigned duties away from the temple, serving as officials and judges over Israel.

When King David was designing plans for his son, Solomon, to build the temple in Jerusalem, "He gave him the plans of all that the Spirit had put in his mind.… He designated the weight of gold for all the gold articles to be used in various kinds of service, and the weight of silver for all the silver articles to be used in various kinds of service" (1 Chronicles 28:12, 14). One key phrase in this passage is "in various kinds of service," which the Spirit had ordained. Just before the temple was completed, Solomon appointed priests, or "church staff," to lead in sacrifices, celebrations, praise, and offerings (treasuries), as well as security guards (gatekeepers) and other workers (2 Chronicles 8:14–16). Believers had ample opportunities for service, just as you probably have ample opportunities at your church today. Some of the church workers were volunteers (not church staff), whose jobs were "to assist the priests according to each day's requirement."

Paul's area of service was as a minister and traveling evangelist: "This is the gospel that you heard. . . . I have become its servant by the commission God gave me" (Colossians 1:23, 25). God may call you, like Paul, into full-time service as a minister or missionary. On the other hand, He may call you to minister in a more informal way, "as you have helped his people and continue to help them" (Hebrews 6:10).

Perhaps you want to serve God in the church kitchen, as a food buyer, or on a hospitality team. "He who supplies seed to the sower and bread for food will also supply and increase your store of seed and will enlarge the harvest of your righteousness. You will be made rich in every way so that...your generosity will result in thanksgiving to God. . . . This service that you perform is not only supplying the needs of God's people but is also overflowing in many expressions of thanks to God" (2 Corinthians 9:10–12). Your giving will enrich your life, overflowing in thanks. God is calling you into His service.

Before Samuel was born, Hannah had prayed for a child who would serve in God's temple. God granted her request, and as soon as she weaned the child, she took him to the temple for full-time service. However, no family member can speak for you in your church service. The time came when God called Samuel individually (1 Samuel 3:1–14). On advice from the priest, Eli, Samuel listened as God spoke to him, saying "Speak, for your servant is listening" (v. 10). Each of us must make the decision Samuel did, regardless of whatever kind of lives our parents have lived. Listen to God's voice yourself, and follow His will. Maturing Christians listen deeply.

❦ **Square Four Ministry: Do an assessment of the world.** Read headlines, survey Web sites, and learn what you can from your own denomination about opportunities for meeting needs around the world. Bruce Wilkinson, his wife, Darlene, their son David, and other family members left opportunities in America (to speak and manage a publishing empire after the popularity of *The Prayer of Jabez* and other books) to go to Africa as God called them. I could hardly believe it when I heard the news, but that's the way God works. I admire the Wilkinsons because they left all—at the height of their popularity—to serve in an obedient way.

Besides full-time missionaries (see www.imb.com and www.namb.net), God needs those in ministry of the Word: translators, computer word processors,

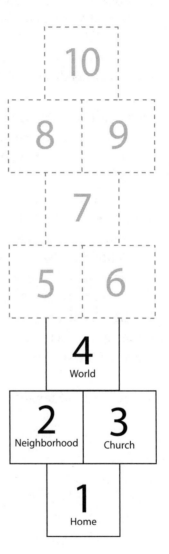

software programmers, publishers, and Christian writers to proclaim the gospel in print. Luke's account of Jesus's birth, which we read at Christmas, has been "handed down to us by those who from the first were eyewitnesses and servants of the word" (Luke 1:2). You can be one who writes what you have witnessed as truth. God also needs evangelists and church planters worldwide. Paul said, "I planted the seed, Apollos watered it, but God made it grow.... The man who plants and the man who waters have one purpose, and each will be rewarded according to his own labor. For we are God's fellow workers" (1 Corinthians 3:6, 8–9).

As I read through a few Psalms this morning, my eye stopped on a metaphor in Psalm 104:4: God compares flames of fire to his servants. (See also Hebrews 1:7, with a reference to angels, God's messengers.) *Are you a flame of fire for God, or has your spark gone out?* Start with a square one ministry and keep looking for opportunities.

In the visual on page 169, fill out squares 5, 6, 7, etc. Draw more squares as you need to define other steps you will take in serving Christ.

What has God taught you, based on this Bible study?

M&M: *Ministry and Missions Moment*

This study has suggested ways to move from square one to wider outreaches into the world. What can you do to bless others after you've done an assessment of each of the hopscotch squares? I know people who have sold their homes, furniture, and cars to move far away to serve God, living on faith. Is God calling you to do the incredible? Though in human or worldly logic, it may be unbelievable, there's a simple answer: whatever God calls you to do, large or small, *do it*. Jesus says, "If anyone gives even a cup of cold water to one of these little ones because he is my disciple, I tell you the truth, he will certainly not lose his reward" (Matthew 10:42).

Deeper Still: *Mystery Revealed*

Here's a deep mystery: *If you cling to your life just as it is, you will lose it. Give yourself away.* Live with your heart open to opportunities for self-giving. "Whoever finds his life will lose it, and whoever loses his life for my sake will find it" (Matthew 10:39).

—— Study 22 ——
Relaying Wisdom

As we have seen in previous studies, it's hard to put a label on what spiritual maturity is. When we see it in someone who's just a little farther along than we are, it invokes curiosity and yearning. If we're wise, we'll try to find out their wisdom and ask them to mentor us. Titus speaks about the mentoring process: "Teach the older women to be reverent in the way they live…to teach what is good. Then they can train the younger women to love their husbands and children, to be self-controlled and pure.... Similarly, encourage the young men to be self-controlled. In everything set them an example by doing what is good" (Titus 2:3–6). Whether you are young or old, you need to be in a Christian mentoring relationship.

As a mature Christian, you care about others, passing along your wisdom. To help them is second nature. Paul says, "For I received from the Lord what I also passed on to you" (1 Corinthians 11:23).

Pass the Baton to a Younger Person

As a young Christian, Kathy Brown once said, "Tell me what it is that makes you a good mentor for somebody like me."

I didn't have a clue.

She said, "I think it's all about giving. You have the spirit of giving."

I thought she was wrong. To me, giving meant stewardship. I thought of the Lottie Moon Christmas Offering in our church. Each year we urge fellow church members to give sacrificially to this offering named after a young missionary to China, Charlotte "Lottie" Moon, who spent her life in sacrifice, finally dying in 1912 after giving her food to hungry Chinese families. To me, *giving* meant a sacrifice of my monetary resources to a worthy cause, such as the Christmas offering—that's all. However, Kathy taught me more about giving. It's a pouring out of your heart, your whole life and your various resources: money, possessions, energy, time, service, courtesy, intelligence, skills, and many others.

Once You Get It, Use Your Spirit of Giving

Kathy has since married a man with older children. As a step-mother, she's poured herself out on behalf of his children, growing to be passionately in love with them as well as him, disciplining only for their good, trying to make wise decisions, and—more than that—trying to *be wise*. When his daughter got married, I watched Kathy work hard: she helped select and buy the dress, made arrangements, and gave many gifts at a sacrifice. Then on the wedding day, she had to sit on a second row while the daughter's mother, who had not helped, sat up front. Kathy said, "I'm learning what love unending means. It's not about me. It's about the spirit of giving. Maybe just about the Spirit...yes, *the* Spirit."

Recently Kathy and I talked. She said, "I get it now—what you've been teaching me for 15 years. Once I got the concept of servanthood, maturity came fast."

Jesus set the example for us in mentoring. He took 12 men and helped them learn about the Christian life. He served as their guide, counselor, teacher, encourager—and even their servant. After a meal with His disciples, Jesus took a towel and a basin and washed His disciples' feet, He said, "Do you understand what I have done for you? You call me 'Teacher' and 'Lord,' and rightly so, for that is what I am. Now that I, your Lord and Teacher, have washed your feet, you also should wash one another's feet. I have set for you an example that you should do as I have done for you" (John 13:12–15). He also gave specific instructions to certain disciples about mentoring. To Simon Peter, he said, "I have prayed for you, Simon, that your faith may not fail. And when you have turned back, strengthen your brothers" (Luke 22:32). The mentoring tradition passed from Christ to Peter (and other disciples), from Peter to the Gentiles, and after hundreds of generations, from one of those Gentiles to me, and from me to Kathy, and from Kathy to the children under her roof, and on to generations to come.

You can seek mentors by reading good books by doctrinally sound writers. As you read, the authors can vicariously mentor you. You might also want to read genealogies, diaries, or memoirs written by godly ancestors in your family or others who offer insight on living the mature Christian life. Over and over in the Bible are these words: "Celebrate this day as a lasting ordinance for the generations to come" (Exodus 12:17). God reminded His people to pass along truths from generation to generation, in the biological family and in the family of God. He is still calling mature Christians to pass the baton in families, through oral or written tradition.

Good Parents? Try Reparenting

In some cases, you may help *reparent* another adult, who has had little training and/or poor examples set before her. In other words, this adult needing help may have had no one to be a real parent to her. Many children grow up with little physical parenting and no spiritual parenting. They are not taught the stages of moral development or self-discipline. Some were abused; some need healing; some need wisdom; some just need your patience. If you had good parents, you have a treasure to share with others. Even if your parents had their faults (we all do), you can share your parents' *good* advice or some counsel they gave that *was* worthwhile for Christian growth. You could also share what you have learned from *your own* experiences and Bible study.

Find a Mentor; Be a Mentor

As you read this study, you may recall godly parents or mentors who guided you in wise choices. Perhaps you've been a Christian since you were young, yet you are seeking to grow more spiritually mature. However, if you did not grow up with good Christian role models, you need to surround yourself with Christian mentors. I believe that every person should *have* a mentor and *be* a mentor to others who are spiritually younger. The Hebrew word *merea* (mah-RAY-ah), feminine form, and *rea* (RAY-ah) masculine form, are used in the Old Testament to refer to *friend*. Today we use the word *merea/rea* to refer to the *one being mentored*, usually a younger friend with whom you can share what you know about life. If you want to become a more mature Christian—no matter what your age—you need a *mentor* to gain wisdom and a *merea*, with whom *you* share *your* knowledge. (For more information, read *Woman to Woman: Preparing Yourself to Mentor* or *Seeking Wisdom: Preparing Yourself to Be Mentored*.) Think of yourself in a middle position, with a spiritually younger seeker looking to you for good advice and godly knowledge and a spiritually older seeker to whom you can look for good advice and godly knowledge.

A year or two ago, I asked a group in Kentucky: "What do you want to know from an older woman like me?"

A young woman responded, "You really want to know?"

"Yes."

"Promise you won't laugh."

"I won't."

"We want to know how to can tomatoes."

Well, yes, I knew how to can tomatoes, but I never dreamed of giving that information to anyone! Who would want it? Canning tomatoes is the hottest, sweatiest job in the world! Tomatoes are harvested in the burning, blistering summertime and boiled over a steamy stove until the canner herself is canned! And here this young woman asked me to teach her to can tomatoes.

Be Not Job Snobs and Disobedient Mentors

Some of us are just God's-job snobs. We may feel some things God has given us to do are beneath us. Sometimes we want to teach what *we* think is significant. We are grumbling, disobedient mentors. Even the most spiritually mature Christians find it hard to be totally giving. Giving our wills to God, for His sake and the sake of others, is hard.

So you want to be a great speaker or evangelist? So you want to be a Christian writer or publisher? So you want to be a wealthy businesswoman? So you want to be an influential godly woman? What are you willing to do to serve God in the meantime, as He is refining you, filling you with good advice and counsel, helping you to learn from others? So you want to work with adults? Begin with children; grow them up in the Lord. So you want to work with well-established people? Start with the destitute; teach the skills they need to become the establishment. So you want a large ministry? Start with two people and lead them to reach others.

So you can't mentor right now because you don't have the education for your task? No excuse. Talk to educators about possibilities. Don't have the time? No excuse. Talk to the busiest person you know to find out how she does it. No one to help you? No excuse. Ask people to pray for you. Form a board of directors for your project. If God clearly tells you to do it and Scriptures support it, you'd better get started. Whatever you do, don't wait. God is moving out in these days. He needs obedient, mature Christians willing to share what they know about Him in whatever way He calls them to be Christ sharers.

Pass the Baton in the Workplace

Today many mature Christians are sharing their knowledge with spiritually younger Christians in creative ways. Several years ago, Henry Blackaby, author of *Experiencing God*, gave an interview. Having spent his life as a pastor and missions leader in the United States and Canada, Blackaby has a unique perspective on the work of God in the US. He says: "I'm hearing a heart cry from the CEOs in the business world. I recently began having a monthly CEO conference call with two men. Just two days ago, we spoke to over 40 in four separate groups, an hour at a time, men from all kinds of Christian faith backgrounds. There is an avalanche of CEOs from major companies—the 'movers and shakers' across the nation—who have heard about this and want to be involved. They want to know, 'How do I relate my relationship to God as a Christian CEO to the workplace?' When we talk with them about the fact that, in the Bible, most all of the activity of God that changed society was done in the workplace and not in the church, suddenly the lights come on and they say, 'How can I then make decisions in the workplace that make a radical difference?'"

Whether you mentor at work, at play, at home, or away, plant a seed. Share your experience with a spiritually younger person who can grow from an immature seed to a mature, sturdy plant in God's kingdom. "He is like a tree planted by streams of water, which yields its fruit in season and whose leaf does not wither" (Psalm 1:3).

M&M: *Ministry and Missions Moment*

I've recognized this mystery as I've lived the Christian life: *Leaders don't just lead; they train leaders.* If you are a Christian leader, your goal is to work yourself out of a job. *Mentor and train someone to take the reins of your ministry.*

Deeper Still: Mystery Revealed

Here's the mystery of mentoring: If you think you have much to share, you probably don't. If you think you have nothing to share, you probably have a wealth of wisdom and experience in your spiritual reservoir. Share it. *Your place of deepest hurt may be the point at which you can bless others.* Meditate on God's will for your service. Don't mentor out of your own strength.

—— Study 23 ——
The Ends of the Earth

This book has been a series of metaphors for the Christian walk. The overriding theme has been that to come out on top in life, a maturing Christian must dive into the deeps, going deeper and deeper still into the mind and heart of God. A second metaphor we've discussed is that being a person of faith is like being a pilgrim on a journey. We've talked about the experience of being distracted from the path, avoiding pot holes, and keeping on the right way to Christian maturity. A third metaphor has been a comparison of the Christian life to a process of growth.

However, the Christian life is also a matter of experience, of recognition that God has grasped you with His grace and love and in that process you have surrendered your life to God. This experience can happen many times as you grow and mature in Christ—but it needs to happen at least once. For most of us, it happens in a moment like the one I call my salvation experience, in which I recognized God for the first time and asked Him into my heart. Paul had such an experience on the road to Damascus when the Spirit of Jesus became real in his life. Then at various times in my Christian life, I've had the opportunity to reacknowledge that I've surrendered my life to Him. As I've matured, I've surrendered more frequently and less dramatically.

Bond with All Humanity

I asked my pastor what he considered traits of a spiritually mature Christian. He said, "They have a bond with all humanity. They are interdependent." Paul, for instance, says he's indebted to others:

I rejoice greatly in the Lord that at last you have renewed your concern for me…. It was good of you to share in my troubles… Even when I was in Thessalonica, you sent me aid…. I have received full payment and even more; I am amply supplied, now that I have received from Epaphroditus the gifts you sent. They are a fragrant offering, an acceptable sacrifice, pleasing to God. (Philippians 4:10, 14, 16, 18)

He calls many of the new Christians in the churches in Asia Minor his "partners" in ministry. He speaks of the times he thanks God in prayer for their partnership. He also has partnership of spirit with people of all kinds: "There is neither Jew nor Greek, slave nor free, male nor female, for you are all one in Christ Jesus. If you belong to Christ, then you are Abraham's seed, and heirs according to the promise…[with] full rights of sons" (Galatians 3:28–29; 4:5). As God accepts all of us, we accept others, without despising their gifts or their sincere understanding. We can correct and advise, but we do not intimidate or hate.

You may be feeling God nudging you to do something for others because you have a special bond with them. You may have met them accidentally, or you may never have met them, yet you feel a strange heart tug to go and tell.

Name several people with whom you have a special bond:

Are you a "hurt magnet"? That is, do people seem drawn to you, seeking help and advice? Is God leading you to begin a ministry of service to them?

Do you ever experience a heart tug for a people group or other category of people? Explain.

Pray that God will make it clear to you how He wants you to respond to the special bond you have with others.

Go to the Ends of the Earth

If the insect on the wall beside my bed had bitten me, I wouldn't have lived to write this book. It looked like knotholes in the beautiful gray wood—until it moved! I was in a jungle in Middle America witnessing to around 100 women at a rustic camp. To tell the truth, it was too rustic for me. When I took a shower, I had to keep my mouth and eyes shut and my ears turned sideways to avoid picking up a parasite in the water that could damage my health for the rest of my life.

A few years later, I stood in a seminary classroom in South America with windows open to the mosquito-filled night. Sweat poured from my body until my clothes were soaked, as I taught a seminar on mentoring. I kept drinking bottled water to replenish and rehydrate. Though I'd put on mosquito repellent since malaria was prevalent among the missionaries there, I was bitten several times.

Another time, in Europe, I was surrounded by guards of an atheistic society, who tore the side panels off our bus, ran mirrors underneath it, and made us get out and hold our passports beside our faces, while guards with machine guns inspected us individually.

I still shudder when I think of these occasions, thanking God I've received His grace. In Middle America, missionaries swatted and killed the "knothole" insect with several brooms! In South America, I never caught a disease from mosquitoes. In Europe, God guided us through the armed checkpoint with just a two-hour delay. Why would I, a city girl, want to go to such remote places? There's only one reason: I want everyone in the world to know Jesus. Because I'm such a softy, I've sacrificed very little compared with those who have given up everything to move to the ends of the earth to tell the world about Christ.

As noted in study 7, many missionaries have given their lives in lonely places for the cause of Christ. While teaching English as a Second Language to internationals in the United States, I met a man from the Afghanistan/Myamar area. He had a sweet spirit and a kind heart. I learned he'd come to America to go to seminary, and he was nearly finished with his degree. One night he came into our church visibly shaken. "Please pray," he said. "I can't get in touch with my family. I've heard there were raids in that area, and my wife and children have no one to protect them. I don't know whether they're alive...or dead." I moved away from that city a few weeks later, never hearing about his family. Yet I have continued to pray for all Christians in that area because I know they are in danger often.

If you know God is not calling you to go overseas to some exotic place to share Jesus, what about a ministry to internationals in your area? Has God brought the world to you, as people from other lands and cultures have moved into your neighborhood? If so, name the groups:

Circle any of the following ministries you might perform:

Teaching conversational English   Hosting a Bible study

Offering driver's training   Helping study for citizenship

Helping secure a job   Teaching health and hygiene

Other (Be specific, as God leads you to write.):

Be Alert to His Voice

One characteristic of maturing Christians is that they are able to hear God's voice. Oswald Chambers wrote, "He [God] looms large tonight. Nothing is worth living for but just Himself." Chambers focused on God as few people have done in their lifetimes. He also wrote, "The gales of the Spirit are blowing over me and conveying something.... I do not distinguish yet. It holds me *strongly alert*." I've used Chambers' words throughout this book, because they are powerful. He went abroad to many places in his short life, because he felt compelled to share Christ.

In Acts 10, God gives us the example of Peter, who went to strangers, crossing a racial barrier, to tell them about God and His plan for salvation. At the beginning of Luke's account in Acts, Peter was spending a few days in the home of Simon the tanner—an untouchable in Jewish culture, because he had to touch dead animals in his work. Peter had already crossed one barrier for clean-living Jews by associating with Simon. While there, he had the same dream three times about unclean food, which he refused, as any decent Jew would, because of God's dietary laws. While he was considering what the dreams may have meant, men knocked at the door, saying their boss, Cornelius, had sent them to ask Peter to come to his house; Cornelius wanted to hear what Peter had to say. Peter went with them over into Europe, shared Jesus with them—and the world was never the same! Peter said, "You are well aware that it is against our law for a Jew to associate with a Gentile or visit him. But God has shown me that I should not call any man impure or unclean" (Acts 10:28). Peter, certainly a mature Christian at this point (though he had been perhaps the most immature of Jesus's disciples earlier), was alert to God's voice. He clearly heard God's call to the Gentiles, and God had given him this special bond with humanity so he could change the world!

Trust God to Provide the Way

The early Church had to make a decision in the coming days about a controversial issue: Could they admit Gentiles? No one had ever done it that way before. It was a hard decision to trust God without all the rules and regulations of their former ceremonies. They had to decide how many of their dietary rules and other dogma should be compulsory. Peter accepted these Gentiles and Cornelius, the Roman centurion who had sent them, just as they were. He preached in that area of Europe, and many were converted. He and Paul advised church leaders to relax the church law, so that Gentiles could be accepted (Acts 15:1–35). After heated debates, they rewrote the rule book (but adhered to the essentials). The Church decided to have mercy on the Gentiles, making it easier for them to become good Christians. And good they were: Cornelius and his family became church leaders of vast influence in the Roman Empire. *Cornelius's influence affirmed the universality of the gospel. Jesus was the Savior of all!*

God still calls evangelists, missionaries, and ordinary Christians, such as you and me, to go and tell. If He is nudging you to go, be alert to His voice. Trust Him; He will provide all you need for the journey.

M&M: *Ministry and Missions Moment*

One thing I've learned about missions that is worthy of sharing is this: *If God calls you to leave everything behind and go to the ends of the earth, He will provide your way.* Financial concerns should not stop you from planning a mission trip or pursuing a career in an entirely different direction from one you have been mired down in for a while. Launch into the deep, knowing God will provide for your needs.

Deeper Still: *Mystery Revealed*

Your *strongly alert* mind is not a tabula rasa; that is, a blank tablet upon which God can write His words—and only His. Instead, your mind is pulled in hundreds of ways, and *you must listen to His voice to separate yourself from the world and to depend on Him.* Keep focused on your Lord.

—— Study 24 ——
Steady Confidence

My mother was a remarkable woman. Growing up in the Great Depression years, she and her family lost two farms they owned and moved into Clinton, South Carolina, to find work in cotton mills. She dropped out of school just before she finished the eleventh grade (the last grade available in high schools in those days) to help support the family. When I was 13, she became the manager of a dress shop in our town, always welcoming customers as family and breaking all records in sales. As my brother, sister, and I grew up, she constantly encouraged us, assuming always we were good, not bad, and leading us in the right direction. She stood tall and erect, often saying, "Edna, stand up straight; hold your shoulders back." On other occasions when I wasn't successful at a given task and said, "I can't," she retorted, "*Can't* never could do anything. Act confident; be confident." She once told me, "Be confident *in Jesus*. I am!" And she was. She would tackle any task and do it well, because she had deep faith and confidence in Jesus.

I'll remember her words all my life: *Be confident in Jesus*. Her confidence spilled over into the lives of her children and grand-children. If I were rating her on a Christian maturity scale, I'd say she was right at the top. Steady confidence in Jesus surely is one of the marks of a mature Christian.

Be Confident in Jesus

The apostle Paul speaks of confidence in seven places in his letter to the Philippians. Paul also says he places his confidence in Jesus, though he has reason to be confident in physical things because of his Jewish heritage: "If anyone else thinks he has reasons to put confidence in the flesh, I have more: circumcised on the eighth day, of the people of Israel, of the tribe of Benjamin, a Hebrew of Hebrews; in regard to the law, a Pharisee; as for zeal, persecuting the church; as for legalistic righteousness, faultless" (Philippians 3:4–6). Paul was born into the favorite tribe of the favorite people of God, the Israelites. By birth and by the law of God, he was perfect. However, he considered all that as loss…rubbish:

But whatever was to my profit I now consider loss for the sake of Christ. What is more, I consider everything a loss compared to the surpassing greatness of knowing Christ Jesus my Lord, for whose sake I have lost all things. I consider them rubbish, that I may gain Christ and be found in him, not having a righteousness of my own that comes from the law, but that which is through faith in Christ. (Philippians 3:7–9)

Be Confident During the Ups and Downs of Life

Paul said, "I can do all things through Christ who strengthens me" (Philippians 4:13 NKJV). *All things* indicates an incredible promise. Missionaries overseas tell of terrible times of danger, yet they didn't fear because God filled them with a confidence of the outcome. Even if they died, they saw they were in God's will and trusted Him in life or in death. John says, "You, dear children, are from God and have overcome them, because the one who is in you is greater than the one who is in the world" (1 John 4:4).

Be Confident Instead of Worrying

Charles was a one-armed mechanic in Alabama, who gave good advice: "I went into the war fearing I'd get hurt. I lost my arm. I feared my daughter wouldn't know me when I returned. She didn't. I feared I'd have no job in civilian life. I had none. Since my family had a history of stroke, I feared having a stroke. I had one, but the last ten years of my life have been worry free. I can honestly say I'm happy; I've learned not to fear tomorrow. Instead of singing, 'When my troubles are so far away, I believe in yesterday,' I sing 'Because He lives, I can face tomorrow.' I replay the joys God's given me. I think of Bible verses, like 'Death where is your sting? Grave, where is your victory?'" The mechanic had more wisdom than many people I know. He said, "You know why God doesn't show us heaven now? Because we're not mature enough to understand it. We couldn't handle the glory of heaven. We'd probably worship it. One day we'll be mature enough to go there."

Pastor Gary Fenton says we believe in one of several oils for our confidence in facing the problems of tomorrow: Oil of Olay covers them over, to be uncovered tomorrow; "Oil of Delay" helps us procrastinate, to protect us from tomorrow; "Oil of Today" gives us joy, to hope for tomorrow; and "Oil of Relay" helps us pass the baton, as we run toward tomorrow.

Be Confident in the Oil of Joy

A man of a faith background different than mine once came over to our table in a restaurant, introduced himself, and said, "You Christians seem so joyful all the time. I've watched you, and you have an air of confidence I don't have." We were able to witness to him, with each Christian at the table confidently speaking the next lines in the Plan of Salvation, and giving our personal testimonies about what God had done in our lives. After he left, we talked about the confidence and joy we have. It's true: Christians do have a deep-down joy because of what Christ did for them. The writer of Hebrews, speaking of Christ, says, "You have loved righteousness and hated wickedness; therefore God, your God, has set you above your companions by anointing you with the oil of joy" (Hebrews 1:9). As we mature, we take on the characteristics of Christ, loving righteousness and hating wickedness, and feeling anointed with the oil of joy.

When the Israelites brought the Ark of the Covenant into Jerusalem, King David, feeling great joy, danced and leaped before the ark (2 Samuel 6:12–22). David made it clear to all those who saw him that he was going to celebrate God! The Christians at Pentecost were so joyous over the infilling of the Holy Spirit that passersby thought they were drunk from wine. Peter explained, using an illustration and these words of David: "I saw the Lord always before me. Because he is at my right hand, I will not be shaken. Therefore my heart is glad.… You have made known to me the paths of life; you will fill me with joy in your presence" (Acts 2:25–26, 28). The oil of joy brings delight: shouting, leaping, and dancing before the Lord. Your joy can fulfill the words of the song,

"I'll Show the World That I'm a Christian." Don't show your confidence by being brash, loud, and bossy. *Wear your delight inside out.*

My mother did not dance. She grew up in a culture that mirrored the Victorian era, when Christians frowned upon such exuberance. How about you? It may have been a long time since you've danced before the Lord. Dance before the Lord today, and *go to dance practice every day.*

Be Confident in God's Word

Read the following verses with positive advice about confidence. Then write in your own words what each passage means:

1 John 2:28

1 John 5:14

1 John 3:21

2 Corinthians 2:3

2 Corinthians 5:6–8

Hebrews 3:14

Read the following warnings about confidence. Then write what each means:

Hebrews 10:35

2 Corinthians 11:17

Proverbs 25:19

What advice would you give to a maturing Christian about his or her confidence?

Be Confident in the Future

Paul says, "We are always confident" (2 Corinthians 5:6). *Always* is a long time. Most Christians are very confident on some days—for instance, just after a spiritual renewal at church—but then other people and worldly thinking weaken their faith. They begin to doubt. Jesus's brother James says, "He who doubts is like a wave of the sea, blown and tossed by the wind" (James 1:6).

Paul has a solution to this lack of confidence: "We live by faith, not by sight" (2 Corinthians 5:7). *Walking in the Spirit of Christ gives a lasting, steady confidence*. Using His power, we can gain confidence for today and tomorrow. "Being confident of this, that he who began a good work in you will carry it on to completion until the day of Christ Jesus" (Philippians 1:6). Mature Christians claim this promise daily, believing that God is working on them, carrying on the work in them until it becomes complete in the day of Christ Jesus. As we have discussed earlier, you don't ever become spiritually mature until the day you go to heaven. There you'll find complete spiritual maturity.

M&M: *Ministry and Missions Moment*

When you order food, do you understand the server's problems when it arrives cold or not cooked according to your instructions? In stores, do you accept service or merchandise that is less than perfect? Does everyone around you know you delight in God? Make it a project this year to magnify the joy on the inside by showing your joy on the outside.

Deeper Still: *Mystery Revealed*

Friedrich Nietzsche, who popularized the "God is dead" theory, remarked that if Christians wanted him to believe in Jesus, they'd have to *show* the joy of Jesus. He believed Christians lacked a delight in their God and showed only sour expressions; he said, "I couldn't believe in a God who didn't dance." God's Word tells us over and over to show joy. After all, the Lord shows his joy over us…with singing: "He will joy over thee with singing" (Zephaniah 3:17 KJV).

Study 25

A Sense of Wonder

On September 11, 2001, I was in Cleveland, Ohio, driving to Columbus—just as a fight occurred over my head aboard United flight 93, which turned at Cleveland and swung over Columbus before crashing in a field just inside Pennsylvania. Without knowing all that was happening in New York, Washington, and Pennsylvania, I stopped in Columbus, visited Christian friends, led a church conference, and finally (after two unexpected nights in an airport hotel watching images of death), drove home to Alabama. Since my heart was broken over the thousands killed in the Twin Towers, I expected to be sad all the way; but as I drove through the Shenandoah Valley, an incredible thing happened. The Holy Spirit came into that rental car in a palpable way. I still remember the joy I experienced. As I began to think of our dear country, God gave me this verse: "But our citizenship is in heaven. And we eagerly await a Savior from there, the Lord Jesus Christ, who, by the power that enables him…[will be able] to bring everything under his control" (Philippians 3:20–21). Even on the darkest days in their lives, maturing Christians can find a sense of wonder in Christ. Kirk Neely says often, "Joy is the infallible proof of the Presence of God in your life."

Hold on to the Wonder

Somehow in all the tragedy in the world—sometimes right on your doorstep—maturing Christians like you hold a sense of the eternal through Jesus Christ. The most unbelievable wonder is that Almighty God loves you and me enough to send His Son to die for us. If we can believe the truth—that He loves us and that nothing we can ever do will make Him stop loving us—then we can believe any miracle He's done throughout history; and God is still performing them today!

Paul's letter to the Romans celebrates the wonder that comes from Christ: "'The Root of Jesse will spring up...the Gentiles will hope in him.' May the God of hope fill you with all joy and peace as you trust in him, so that you may overflow with hope by the power of the Holy Spirit" (15:12–13). As immature Christians we sometimes fail to secure the wonder in our hearts and memories. Whatever you do, remember to hold on to the wonder.

Toss the Mold Aside

A sense of the amazing creativity and innovation that comes from the Father will enable maturing Christians to toss the mold aside; that is, to forget the rut they're in and begin a new creative enterprise based on faith in their creative Creator. Just as the Root of Jesse, that is, *Christ*, sprang up, bringing new life, you can begin a fresh start, a creative ministry or lifestyle. Within you is the spark of creativity that only the Savior can give. Because you were born in the image of God, you have a certain godliness inside you. The pattern of the world does not have to mold you, but *you can become a new creature in Christ, new every morning.* Pray for God's help in following His pattern for your life.

Forget the Old Blunder

Paul prays often for his fellow Christians, knowing God commands us to work with others in unity: "May the God who gives endurance and encouragement give you a spirit of unity among yourselves as you follow Christ Jesus, so that with one heart and mouth you may glorify the God and Father of our Lord Jesus Christ" (Romans 15:5–6). Sounds easy, doesn't it? Yet working with people is always a precarious journey. As you walk the path to Christian maturity, you will also find problems with personalities or temperaments. I don't know what kind of problems you've had in your church or with other Christians, but I am quite certain you have experienced some difficulties. You make blunders; they make blunders. Pride, misreading body language, and misunderstanding spoken words cause hurt in the body of Christ. Walking in tandem with other Christians is not easy.

Paul says, "Accept one another, then, just as Christ accepted you, in order to bring praise to God. For I tell you that Christ has become a servant of the Jews on behalf of God's truth, to confirm the promises made to the patriarchs so that the Gentiles may glorify God for his mercy" (Romans 15:7–10). Notice that we are to forgive as Christ forgave us. (See similar words in the model prayer Jesus provided.) The greatest blunder is our spiritual condition since the Fall in Eden: because we are conceived in sin and born in sin (Psalm 51:5), we grow up in sin and guilt, and they are dissolved only when we invite Jesus into our hearts to indwell us, which is the greatest wonder of all. Oswald Chambers said, "I am so amazed that God has altered me that I can never despair of anybody."

Even after they have found Him as Savior, immature Christians live with guilt, but when we realize that God sent His Son to earth to become a servant on our behalf (Romans 15:8), we can find peace in God's mercy. As he forgives us, we *forget* sin against us after we *forgive* it (Hebrews 8:12).

One of the joys of forgetting old blunders (our sins or the sins of others) is *celebrating with awe the feeling of starting over again*. With a sense of gratefulness, we thank God. Notice verse 9 of Romans 15: "Glorify God for his mercy." God says, "Sing praises to him, all you peoples" (v. 11).

Read Romans 15:7–10.

How many different people groups do you find and who are they?

For which two reasons does Paul say you should forgive others and accept their shortcomings?

1.

2.

For which two reasons did Christ have to become a servant?

1.

2.

Review Romans 15:5–6. How can you show others you're willing to become a servant to other Christians for the unity of believers?

Are you still harboring unforgiveness in your heart for anyone in your life? If so, write their initials here:

If you know you have forgiven, but you have trouble *forgetting*, what suggestions could you give someone to help the person in a similar struggle? Write down three things a person who has been wronged can do to erase those memories:

Share these suggestions with others who may have the same problem.

Remember, no one is perfect, not even the most mature Christian in the world today. Based on your experience, help others to accept themselves as imperfect—as all of us are—and encourage them in their forgiving and forgetting.

Be Bold in Your Thunder

Paul says, "I have written you quite boldly on some points, as if to remind you of them again, because of the grace God gave me to be a minister of Christ Jesus...proclaiming the gospel of God" (Romans 15:15–16). When you focus on the grace God has given you to serve Him, you can do nothing but speak boldly. One important phrase is "the grace God gave me to be a minister." You probably know ministers who love to preach from a church pulpit, feeling compelled to speak loudly and clearly: "God is love! God is love!" They can hardly keep silent, when they have opportunity to speak. Whatever God has given you as a passion, He will enable you to serve Him through that passion and give you a sense of wonder when He allows you to use it to bless others.

The Wonder of a Blessing

Part of the wonder of a maturing Christian is the abundance of blessings that God gives. You can expect blessings! They come in several kinds:

1. *The Common Blessing,* which Adam and Eve experienced in the garden of Eden, expressed in the goodness in the world
2. *The Behavior Blessing* on earth: the mercy and grace God gives as a reward for doing good
3. *The Conversion Blessing,* which you obtain in heaven, where there are many blessings—just by being a believer
4. *The Compensation Blessing,* for things you give on earth, which you receive as a reward for your unselfishness
5. *The Compassion Blessing* to all who ask, based on the generosity of God's character; He loves to give us things, the greatest of which was His only Son (John 3:16).

A blessing is personal, not external but internal. We don't tell God exactly how to bless us. We pray for special blessings and then let Him direct how He wants to give them.

A blessing is also directed by God, abundant and infinite. Its fullness goes on forever.

What Can I Do to Bless God?

God's blessings are not on a one-way street. You can bless God by doing the following:

1. Ask God daily for blessings.
2. List blessings and thank God for each one.
3. Enjoy each blessing (1 Timothy 6:17).
4. Share your blessings (1 Timothy 6:18).
5. Seek long-lasting honor and blessings from God.

David said, "Bless the LORD, O my soul; and all that is within me, bless His holy name. Bless the LORD, O my soul, and forget not all his benefits" (Psalm 103:1–2 NKJV). As you hold on to the wonder, praise Him all the way to heaven, where you'll feel at home. *Thanksgiving is the language of heaven* (Revelation 5:11–12).

M&M: *Ministry and Missions Moment*

It's hard to hold on to the wonder if you're too traditional to toss the mold aside, too guilty to forget the old blunders, and too timid to be bold in your thunder for the cause of Christ. If you're so bound in your life that you can't bless God through your service for Him today, remember, *God will never lead you where His grace can't cover you!* Claim blessings # 2 and # 4 soon. God will give you all the rest without you even trying.

Deeper Still: *Mystery Revealed*

Being bold in your thunder should not be confused with being angry, caustic, or loud and rude toward others. Righteous indignation is no excuse for losing your temper or losing control. Here's a mysterious principle of God: *The deeper you go in His wonder, the softer your temper is.* The more you grow in His joy, the more you speak out—but not in a thundering manner—in a soft, winsome voice. *Your wonder holds soft thunder.* Spend time praising God in a whisper.

Unit 6

———————— ● ————————

PRAISE GOD FROM WHOM ALL BLESSINGS FLOW

All of me is gone, my King; my life be You alone.
All You, with heaven blazing, brightly leading, true and clear.

Heaven is near; I see the lights. The signs grow deeper still
As all of us, Dear King, bow down and pray around the throne.

And then arise and one by one we waft on Spirit's wings
To serve, to think, to understand, to meld in you, O Lamb.

"Shh! Rest, My child, My best," the heavenly Voice flows
    deeper still.
I see His face and He sees mine. I slow, I stop, I rest.

Study 26
Total Submission

The day we buried my husband, one of the pallbearers, "Jerry," came to tell me this story. A few years before, he'd lost a child, Taylor, who died accidentally on the first day Jerry had taken care of him all day. Snow had counseled with Jerry many times, and they'd sat under the stars at night in the yard, talking about life and death. At Snow's interment, Jerry saw a child's grave marker nearby, which reminded him of his deceased son. Suddenly he felt a pat on the shoulder. He turned to say, "Thank you; I'm all right" to whoever it was who knew how close he was to Snow. No one was within ten feet of him.

As he looked again at the child's monument, he heard a whisper, "You can come on home now, son. I've straightened out everything with Taylor."

As Jerry told me this story, he said, "Edna, to tell the truth, I haven't wanted to go to heaven. My heart was so heavy with guilt when I thought of Taylor. He trusted me, and I let him down. I didn't want to face him in heaven. He might ask, "Where were you, Dad, when I needed you most?" In the past few months, I've tried to do everything I could to make God quit loving me enough to kick me out of heaven…quit going to church…did some really bad things. I think the first thing Snow did when he got to heaven was to look Taylor up and explain on my behalf. Now, I'm ready to go." Jerry lost the guilt and depression. He came alive in ministry because he became totally submissive to Christ. Because he believed "All things work together for good to them that love God, to them who are the called according to his purpose" (Romans 8:28

KJV), he began counseling others whose children had died.

James said, "Count it all joy when ye fall into various trials; knowing that the testing of your faith produces patience" (James 1:2 NKJV). New Testament Christians celebrated their sacrifice. "Now if we are children, then we are heirs—heirs of God and co-heirs with Christ, if indeed we share in his sufferings in order that we may also share in his glory" (Romans 8:17).

Read Philippians 3:10–11. What kind of fellowship does Paul mention?

What five things does God say He wants you to do?

1. To know _____ .

2. To know the power of His _____ .

3. To know the fellowship of sharing in _____ .

4. To become like _____ in His _____ .

5. To attain to the _____ from the _____ .

In your opinion, what does suffering accomplish? Explain:

Activities of Total Submission

Total Submission Shares in Jesus' Suffering

Jesus, of course, gave the ultimate sacrifice. No one has suffered worse than He, since He not only was crucified in the most horrible way, but also took on the burden of all the sin in the world, when for a little while, the Holy God turned His back on the ungodly sin that permeated His Son on the cross. Mary Ann Ward Appling, former *Contempo* magazine editor, once wrote, "When you find yourself in the hot seat sharing your faith, remember Jesus was there first." He suffered more than you will ever suffer, loved you more than you will ever love Him, and is our example of total submission—to death for your sake.

Total Submission Satisfies God's Heart

When you share in His suffering, you choose to pour yourself out as an acceptable sacrifice, which has a sweet-smelling savor for Him. "For we are to God the aroma of Christ" (2 Corinthians 2:15). At the Samaritan well, Jesus said, "I thirst. Give me drink." You can satisfy Christ's longing for relationship with you. Oswald Chambers said, "May my Lord never let me grow cold in my longing to be a cup in His hand for the quenching of His own royal thirst."

Total Submission Celebrates the Sacrifice

As strange as it may seem to a nonbeliever, maturing Christians know that their total submission and obedience satisfies God's heart. For the joy of relationship with Him, they don't see submission and obedience as a horrible sacrifice. C. S. Lewis said, as his wife was dying of bone cancer, *"You never know how much you really believe anything until its truth or falsehood becomes a matter of life and death to you."* During the pain and suffering of life, as you mature in your relationship with Christ, you celebrate the suffering as a time of total submission, which leads to revelation, fellowship, and utter dependence upon the nurturing God. According to Philip Yancey, the nonbeliever "fights pain like Hercules' cutting off the Hydra's head, while new writhing expressions of suffering emerge." However, the maturing Christian, in an act of complete surrender, embraces whatever God gives, yielding to the Master's will.

Jolene Ivy, a cancer survivor, said what I've heard many other crisis survivors say: "I would not want to go back to the place where I was spiritually before I knew I had cancer. God has given me a spiritual blessing that is unbelievable and priceless; He's also used the illness for me to bless others through my testimony of His goodness." If you are thinking, *Such a person is not facing reality; they're avoiding the disappointment of admitting they're dying,* then think again. This celebration is real.

Total Submission Embraces Deeper Baptism in the Death of Jesus

Read Galatians 2:20: "I am crucified with Christ; nevertheless I live; yet not I, but Christ liveth in me (KJV). Andrew Murray once said about this verse: "He is the Crucified Son of God. Of all the characteristics of conformity, this must be the chief and most glorious one: conformity to His death.... Conformity to Christ's death is the power to keep us from the power of sin.... The cross means entire self-denial"—total submission.

Celebration and Actualization

People like Jolene are operating at Coburg's stage 6 of moral development. Abraham Maslow, who designed a pyramid for the hierarchy of human needs, called his top level of self-sufficiency "self-actualization," in which a person's selfish human needs are diminished. I believe maturing Christians have reached this level—regardless of how it is labeled by the world.

Oswald Chambers wrote of being stripped before God:

It took me a long while to realize that God has no respect for anything I bring Him. All He wants from me is unconditional surrender.... I will have faith in God while He shows me my ignorance, my mistakes,

my weakness, and takes away all my shallow creduli-
ties I used to call faith. I asked Him for patience, and
one after another he takes away my prospects of suc-
cess. By the means of the keen criticism of experts, He
has lifted the veil to show me how I have tried to
express my thoughts.

God stripped Chambers bare before Him, and brought him to sanctification, holiness, and spiritual maturity. In study 20, we discussed
the suffering you once hated, but which you now realize has led you
to obedience and intimacy with God. The writer of Hebrews told
us that Jesus learned obedience through suffering (Hebrews 5:8).
Though you look forward to eternal life, *you're willing to suffer for
the joy of knowing Jesus, whether you receive a reward or not.* You truly
become a brother or sister in the family of God, with your Brother,
Jesus Christ.

What is your favorite quote from Oswald Chambers?

Why?

**How will you seek conformity in Christ (Andrew Murray's suggestion
on page 203)?**

Write steps you will take this year to surrender unconditionally to Him:

The ALL Principle

In speaking of Martha of Bethany, Kimberly Sowell, says, "God doesn't want us committed; he wants us *surrendered*." There's a big difference. Like Martha, we may be a hard worker in the church, a committed Christian, but God wants everything! He wants us obedient in *all* things (2 Corinthians 2:9), especially obedient to the faith (Romans 1:5), obedient to truth through the Spirit (1 Peter 1:22), obedient unto righteousness (Romans 6:16), obedient in our thoughts (2 Corinthians 10:5–6), obedient to God's voice (Joshua 22:2), obedient to God's commands (Jeremiah 35:18), and obedient in our nation (1 Samuel 15:22). In summary, *Jesus wants it all. He will accept nothing less.*

The old hymn I sang as a child says, "Jesus paid it all. All to Him I owe." We owe Him everything: our deliverance, our assurance, our reliance, our alliances, and finally our acquiescence to His omniscience, omnipotence, and omnipresence.

M&M: *Ministry and Missions Moment*

This study has explored many Scriptures about sacrifice. Samuel said to King Saul, "To obey is better than sacrifice" (1 Samuel 15: 22). Paul says the Romans obeyed "from the heart" (Romans 6:17 KJV) or "wholeheartedly" (NIV), and then he tells them such obedience will be rewarded: "Now that you have been set free from sin and have become slaves to God, the benefit you reap leads to holiness, and the result is eternal life" (Romans 6:22). Has God been calling you to a ministry that demands total surrender? Why have you hesitated? *If God demands total surrender, obey.*

Deeper Still: *Mystery Revealed*

Based on today's study, pray this prayer today: "O God, baptize me deeper into the suffering and death of Jesus. Strengthen my soul for communion with You. Help me deny self and receive the victory that only You can give me. Amen."

Find a hymnbook today and sing the stanza in "Blessed Assurance" that begins: *"Perfect submission, all is at rest."*

—— Study 27 ——
Successful Mistakes

My sister, Phyllis, one of the most godly women I know, purposefully goes on a mission trip yearly. Last summer she shared a state list of opportunities with adults and teens in her church and then went with a group on a mission trip to Charleston, South Carolina. They worked in a variety of places, cheering up lonely people by giving manicures in a nursing home and an assisted living facility, giving out Scripture portions, and witnessing. In a beautiful park with dozens of tourists, as the group was busy sharing Scriptures and offering cool water, Phyllis noticed a lady standing by the water cooler, but not drinking water.

"Can we help you?" Phyllis asked.

"My husband just died," blurted the lady. "They just told me...."

Phyllis stopped what she was doing. Realizing this lady needed her immediately, she tenderly comforted her as only Phyllis can, crying with her and encouraging her. Later (again while they were busy) they gave water to a man who seemed disoriented. When they asked what was wrong, he told them he was a stranger in Charleston, where his wife had been sent for medical care at the University of South Carolina Medical Center. His wife had been transferred by ambulance from that hospital to another one; he had taken a taxi that left him on the wrong corner. In that bustling urban area he had no idea where the hospital was. Phyllis helped him find the right building and asked if he needed water. He took both kinds, cool water for his throat and living water for his soul. The taxi driver had made a mistake, but God used it for a successful movement of the Holy Spirit as Phyllis was alert to spiritual needs.

Pay Attention to God's Parentheses

Oswald Chambers says, "God puts a parenthesis in the middle flow of our life." Pay attention to it. In study 14 we considered times when you are sidetracked—detoured from your godly purpose. However, some detours are actually *godly parentheses*. When you're working hard at a task, going down the righteous road, and something interrupts you, you may think it's a mistake, but if you're alert, you'll recognize God's parenthesis in your day.

I once had a flat tire on my way to a church conference. I was impatient. The mechanic fixed the flat and found something wrong with the axle. I approved the repair, urging him to hurry. Time was ticking. The mechanic made a mistake and had to order another part. By then I knew I was going to be late. I did miss the entire conference that day, but—thank God—I finally recognized the parenthesis in the flow of my life and was able to give a full presentation of the gospel to an unchurched man: the mechanic! Another time I was witnessing to a man on a plane when the flight attendant kept interrupting. As it turned out, she was the one who needed to hear the gospel! (I found out only after the flight that

I was really witnessing to *her*. Her life was changed in what might be called a "holy coincidence," and I didn't have a clue this was God's parenthesis in my life that day.)

A friend puts it succinctly: "When you are uptight, just slow down, pay attention to the *God signs*. Just trust God and do the next thing!"

Have you ever experienced times when you saw God signs in a situation that seemed like a disaster or a mistake? If so, explain:

Have you ever noticed God putting a parenthesis in the middle flow of your life?

Share your experiences with a study partner or friend.

The Temptation of Success

Because God seems to bring blessing out of disaster and "everything turns out all right," maturing Christians may fall into the trap of thinking they'll never fail because they're in the center of God's will. Being a partner with God in leading the world to Christ can rouse a heady feeling of importance. You may say within yourself: *I'm a humble Christian, and proud of it!* Because we are human, we get excited and begin to revel in our personal success.

Here are four warnings about handling success, especially the temptation to celebrate self:

❦ **Avoid excess pride.** Pride will come, because Satan uses pride as a tool to trip you up. As soon as you recognize any sign of pride, weed it out. Come back to center. *Dive deeper into humility.* Give God the glory for all successes.

❦ **Focus on others, not self.** Besides focusing on God, a wholesome focus on others and their needs will keep yours from looming large. *Dive deeper into ministry.*

❦ **Remain in constant contact with your leader, God Himself.** Spend time in prayer and meditation on what you already know of Him. *Dive deeper into prayer.*

❦ **Quote Scriptures.** God's Word ingrained in your mind and soul will surface when you need it most. It can keep you from a multitude of sins (Hebrews 4:12–13). Memorize as much of it as you can. *Dive deeper into His Word.*

Paul says, "For by the grace given me I say to every one of you: Do not think of yourself more highly than you ought, but rather think of yourself with sober judgment" (Romans 12:3). Anchor yourself in Christ. No matter how deeply you love your Lord, going still deeper (*still* and *deeper*) gives you power to maintain control of your soaring spirit.

How do you handle success? List some things you've done after a successful day:

Write the following Scriptures in your own words, as they apply to your life:

"To fear the LORD is to hate evil; I hate pride and arrogance" (Proverbs 8:13).

"Pride goes before destruction, a haughty spirit before a fall" (Proverbs 16:18).

"This is the one I esteem: he who is humble and contrite in spirit, and trembles at my word" (Isaiah 66:2).

The Mystery of God's Parentheses

From early times God's people, walking in the flesh, were unable to see spiritual truths. Moses called all the Israelites to renew the covenant with God, reminding them of all the miracles they had seen in Egypt and during the Exodus through the wilderness: "But to this day the LORD has not given you a mind that understands or eyes that see or ears that hear" (Deuteronomy 29:4).

If you've ever wondered why Christian precepts seem so easy for some to comprehend and hard for others, you are not alone. Jesus's disciples asked the same kind of questions. Matthew 13 records Jesus telling a parable ending with, "He who has ears, let him hear"

(v. 9). His disciples asked, "Why do you speak to the people in parables?" (v. 10). Jesus answered, "The knowledge of the secrets of the kingdom of heaven has been given to you, but not to them" (v. 11). Lingering in His presence, the disciples had moved deeper into the heart and mind of Christ. They were able to discern spiritual truth, unlike those Jewish leaders with impure hearts who were trying to trick Jesus—those who lived by the letter of the law without spiritual discernment.

In his letter to Christians in Rome, Paul says, "I do not want you to be ignorant of this mystery, brothers, *so that you may not be conceited*" (Romans 11:25, italics added), that is, tempted to be puffed up with self-importance over your own spiritual understanding and success. Paul might have said these words, echoed in the twenty-first century: "It's not about you; it's about Him." It's *God's will* that Gentiles would be saved, and then *in God's timing* that the Jews will be saved. All people must turn from trying to obey the Old Testament Law, which serves as a mirror to show them their own sin. Once they realize the futility of trying to save themselves through obeying the Law perfectly, then they are humbled, ready to believe that Jesus died for their sins and open to ask Him to come into their hearts. Paul explains,

Israel has experienced a hardening in part until the full number of the Gentiles has come in. And so all Israel will be saved, as it is written [a prediction from Isaiah 27:9, 13]: 'The deliverer will come from Zion [the Jerusalem hill where God's temple was located]; he will turn godlessness away from Jacob [Jacob's descendants: Jews]. And this is my covenant with them when I take away their sins'. As far as the gospel is concerned, they are enemies on your account [unbelievers who've rejected Jesus]; but as far as election is concerned, they are loved on account of the patriarchs, for God's gifts and his call are irrevocable. Just as you who were at one time disobedient to God have now received mercy as a result of their disobedience [Jewish leaders led the attack on Jesus, who died for your sins], so they too have now become disobedient in order that they too may now receive mercy as a result of God's mercy to you. (Romans 11:25–31)

Christ died for everybody who will believe in Him: whether born Gentile, Jew, Greek, Roman, American, or British; male or female; young or old; all those from Hindu, Muslim, Taoist, Buddhist, atheistic, and Christian homes. Everybody.

How can you be alert to the unlikely *everybodies* of the world? List practical ways you can be alert to possible opportunities for witnessing:

Ever since the early Christian church era in the first century, we are inheritors of this mystery, now revealed.

We speak of God's secret wisdom, a wisdom that has been hidden and that God destined for our glory before time began. None of the rulers of this age understood it, for if they had, they would not have crucified the Lord of glory. However, as it is written: 'No eye has seen, no ear has heard, no mind has conceived what God has prepared for those who love him'—but God has revealed it to us by the Spirit. The Spirit searches all things, even the deep things of God. (1 Corinthians 2:7–10).

We must be aware of spiritual parentheses—these "deep things" that flow into our lives. If we live in the Spirit, we can see the mystery revealed in Scripture and in our everyday lives.

Now to him who is able to establish you by my gospel and the proclamation of Jesus Christ, according to the revelation of the mystery hidden for long ages past, but now revealed and made known through the prophetic writings by the command of the eternal God, so that all nations might believe and obey him—to the only wise God be glory forever through Jesus Christ! Amen. (Romans 16:25–27)

M&M: Ministry and Missions Moment

The Holy Spirit is not *esoteric*, that is, meant to be understood only by a small, intelligent group. The Spirit is practical as He works in your life. He lets every Christian know how and what to do to please God in everyday life. Furthermore, as they flow in and out of your day, *the parentheses of life are open-ended.* God allows you free will to choose how they end, how you will answer successful mistakes as they pop up often. You choose: with an irritated attitude, with spiritual discernment, with a prideful ego, or with a grateful heart.

Deeper Still: *Mystery Revealed*

Here's a mystery that maturing Christians understand: *God is constantly at work in you, just out of sight.* You'll be amazed in heaven when you learn all the things God has done. Occasionally, through Jesus, the veil is lifted so you can see the Spirit's work: a tardy schedule that saved your life, a detour that brought spiritual rewards, or an illness that gave you spiritual joy beyond measure. Today meditate on the times God's detours or sudden parentheses flowed into your life. Celebrate those you do understand and contemplate those you don't, looking forward to complete revelation when you know even as you are known (1 Corinthians 13:12 paraphrased).

—— Study 28 ——
Respect for Gifts

An older church member, "Mary," went to take a gift to her deacon at his home. His small daughter, Jenny, opened the door.

"Will you call your father?"

"Yep.... Daaaaaaddy!" she screamed. "There's an old lady here to see you!"

They waited. Finally, Jenny looked up at the older woman, then down all the way to her feet.

"Daddy, you'd better hurry! She's really old."

When the father came, of course, he tried to apologize, but there was no missing the point: Mary must not have much time left! She was *really* mature. Sometimes people put false designations on older people, assuming that age makes them nicer, wiser, and "spiritual-er"! These things are not always true. For instance, an older person is not necessarily spiritually mature. Often a 15-year-old Christian who's attended church training for years may be more spiritually mature than a 75-year-old new Christian or one who has never gone to any kind of Bible study or spiritual training to help develop her relationship with Christ.

On the other hand, sometimes young people don't have much respect for older people; their fashions are out of date, their electronic devices are obsolete, and their houses are a little musty. The truth is that most Christians my age have experienced the ups and downs of life and have learned many things from trial and error. In addition, they have learned spiritual truths through prayer, Bible study, and the interaction with other maturing Christians. Here is one thing I have experienced: As years advance, you advance your understanding, accept your spiritual gifts, and begin using those things God's given you in life to bless the lives of others, little by little understanding His will for you. You also accept the gifts of others as equally important as yours.

Have you ever judged someone based on their age, as Jenny did? If so, write about the encounter:

Different Gifts, but the Same Spirit

God tells us that each one of us is given at least one spiritual gift at the time of salvation. It is up to us to use that gift in the kingdom of God. (If you've never taken a spiritual gifts inventory, do so now by taking the inventory in *Yours for the Giving* by Barbara Joiner, available from www.newhopepublishers.org or www.wmustore.com.) Paul lists spiritual gifts in several places. To the church at Rome, he says: "We have different gifts, according to the grace given us. If a man's gift is *prophesying*, let him use it in proportion to his faith. If it is *serving*, let him serve; if it is *teaching*, let him teach; if it is *encouraging*, let him encourage; if it is *contributing to the needs of others*, let him give generously; if it is *leadership*, let him govern diligently; if it is *showing mercy*, let him do it cheerfully" (Romans 12:6–8).

In 1 Corinthians 12, Paul explains spiritual gifts to the church at Corinth: "Now about spiritual gifts, brothers, I do not want you to be ignorant.... There are different kinds of gifts, but the same Spirit. There are different kinds of service, but the same Lord. There are different kinds of working, but the same God works all of them in all men. Now to each one the manifestation of the Spirit is given for the common good" (vv. 1, 4–7). Then he lists the following gifts: *the message of wisdom, the message of knowledge, faith, gifts of healing, miraculous powers, prophecy, distinguishing between spirits, speaking in different kinds of tongues, and interpretation of tongues.* Paul makes it clear that the Spirit "gives them to each one, just as he determines" (v. 11). Then he lists other gifts, some of which overlap: *apostles, prophets, teachers, workers of miracles, those having gifts of healing, and those speaking in different kinds of tongues* (v. 28), following with an explanation of their use (1 Corinthians 14:1–40). Maturing Christians are usually familiar with these gifts and respect gifts of the Spirit in others.

Of the gifts in italic print, which one do you think is your passion, or spiritual gift?

Which gifts do you admire most?

Which gifts do you respect in others, but you have little interest in them?

How can you affirm gifts in others who are different from you?

Your Gift Is as Good as Mine

One of the most important characteristics of a mature Christian is that he avoids gift despisement, that is, looking down on others' gifts—not accepting all spiritual gifts as equal. Whether they admit it or not, many Christians feel the gifts they possess (or others whom they admire, such as great preachers or religious leaders, possess) are superior to the gifts some other Christians possess. I have several charismatic friends, for instance, who feel they have a special touch from God because they speak in unknown tongues. They are quick to quote Paul's words, "I thank God that I speak in tongues more than all of you" (1 Corinthians 14:18), and refer to "full-gospel" churches as if mainline Christian denominations are not believers in a complete gospel. To be truthful, sometimes noncharismatic Christians feel inferior. On the other hand, I have non-charismatic friends who quote the next verse in 1 Corinthians 14: "But in the church I would rather speak five intelligible words to instruct others than ten thousand words in a tongue" (v. 19), implying that charismatics' gift of tongues is unintelligible. Paul makes it clear we are not to despise one another's gifts: "There should be no division in the body, but that its parts should have equal concern for each other" (1 Corinthians 12:25). Though we may not agree, we should be able to say without prejudice or jealousy, "Your gift is as good as mine," and avoid gift despisement.

No gift despisement was the rule of the characters in Frank Baum's *Wizard of Oz.* All the characters in that work had parts missing: The scarecrow had no brain. The lion had no courage. The tin man had no heart. The characters who went down the yellow brick road depended on each other for encouragement. All of us have parts missing, just as they did. We accept that some of our brothers and sisters who love Jesus have different spiritual gifts, which God has given them. He made them every bit as good as we are.

Read 1 Corinthians 12:1–3, 12–31. Which part of the body can you identify with?

Why?

Lack of a Mean or Critical Spirit

Another characteristic of a mature Christian is that he or she avoids a mean or critical spirit. I feel quite uncomfortable around Christians who are so passionate about certain doctrines that they are argumentative and condescending toward others. This semester at a Christian university where I teach, I watched one professor follow a student out the door, shaking his fist and speaking in a demanding voice: "No, your tolerance makes you wrong. I'm a warrior; you're afraid to take a stand. If you have any backbone, you must boycott...." People with mean or critical spirits have few places in the halls of Christian maturity. God is love, and the language of His people is love.

Alexander Whyte said, "Oh, the unmitigated curse of controversy! Eschew controversy as you would eschew the entrance to hell itself! Let them have it their own way. Let them talk, let them write, let them correct you, let them traduce you. Let them judge and condemn you, let them slay you. Rather let the truth of God itself suffer than that love suffer. You have not enough of the Divine nature in you to be a controversialist." Screaming, criticizing, and coercing are not the tools of a spiritually mature person. I believe we should defend the principles of God, and I would be willing to die for some of them, but a good measure of spiritual maturity is a quiet spirit, a forgiving nature, and a peace-loving ability to control your temper and criticism. Jesus said, "Blessed are the merciful, for they will be shown mercy.... Blessed are the peacemakers, for they will be called sons of God" (Matthew 5:7, 9).

The Golden Rule

We learned in study 10 that only people at the deepest level of moral development are able to live by the Golden Rule. I know people who absolutely despise anyone who is different from them. Even people who proclaim to be Christians fear and hate people from the other side of the world who claim Christians are their enemies, just because the foreign group has proclaimed its hatred for us. The more mature you are in your spiritual walk, the more you are able to live by the Golden Rule, and to form this sympathetic bond with all humanity. Jesus said, "Love your enemies and pray for those who persecute you" (Matthew 5:44).

Showing Your Respect for Others' Spiritual Gifts

Maturing Christians behave in several obvious ways that show they have no gift despisement.

1. Look eye to eye. You don't look down in a condescending way or up in a fearful way, but straight across the table, at eye level with others.

2. Harbor no prejudice of strangers. That is, you don't prejudge or fear the unknown about a person you don't know just because of what you see at first glance or hear from other prejudiced people. You replace racial or cultural prejudice with an openness of heart. When Peter left Joppa for Caesarea and eventually Europe, his openness to Gentiles changed the world forever (Acts 10).

3. Ask for help. The parable of the good Samaritan becomes more compelling when you consider that the Jews identified, not with the good Samaritan, but with the man in the ditch. You must be willing to let others help you, especially with their own gifts, accepting those gifts as valid, and accepting your own vulnerability before them.

4. Issue outlandish hospitality. Jesus dined with the worst sort of people: publicans (guilty of tax fraud), sinners (guilty of defaming their bodies and souls), scribes and Pharisees (guilty of heresy and misuse of power), and harlots and outcasts. The early Church welcomed everybody.

5. Go wherever God tells you to go, even to help people you think don't deserve helping. After he got out of the great fish's stomach, Jonah witnessed to people in Nineveh, but it set his teeth on edge to hear of their salvation. He hated them, and felt God wasted His great love on such a sinful, pitiful people.

Which of the behaviors (# 1–5) that show no gift despisement seems easiest for you to do?

Why did you choose that item?

How does it fit your lifestyle?

M&M: *Ministry and Missions Moment*

As a maturing Christian, go one step further past *gift acceptance*. Actively use your gifts to encourage the gifts of others. That's what ministry and missions are all about. Help others see that the first step for finding and using their spiritual gifts is accepting the Holy Spirit of God, the creator of all gifts, into their heart. As you lead others to come to know Jesus and discover their gifts, you are delivering the message of reconciliation: "God was reconciling the world to himself in Christ, not counting men's sins against them. And he has committed to us the message of reconciliation" (2 Corinthians 5:19).

Deeper Still: Mystery Revealed

The disciples came to Jesus, saying, "Rabbi, where are you staying?" Jesus said, "Come, and you will see" (John 1:36–39). Jesus issued this simple invitation to all people. Here's the mystery: *Jesus's invitation to salvation is the most simple invitation, yet has the most profound consequences.* It is a life-and-death invitation. He stretches out His hand, always waiting for your RSVP, waiting to have a deeper relationship with you. He says, "Here I am! I stand at the door and knock. If anyone hears my voice and opens the door, I will come in" (Revelation 3:20). As you meditate today on His Word, open your heart's door. Ask Him in, for a deeper relationship.

—— Study 29 ——
A Leadership of One

Born in eighteenth-century England, William Carey grew to be a courageous man who went *deeper, deeper still* into spiritual maturity. As a young man, he made shoes in a small cobbler shop in Moulton, England, where he drew a world map on a wall, indicating how many "pagans" were in each country. For instance, he wrote on the eastern United States: Cherokee, 168,000 pagans; Choctaw, 76,000 pagans; etc. When I visited that small cobbler shop in 1990, I saw similar statistics on the plastered wall. Across from that wall sat an anvil, a cobbler's stool, and a built-in vat for soaking leather. In this small room, Carey had made the shoes that he carried on foot to Kettering, the nearest city, 19 miles away, where he sold them.

As Martin Luther several hundred years before him and as Peter and Paul, who had stepped outside *their* comfort zones, Carey was a courageous trailblazer. Belonging to a group of Baptist dissenters shunned by many traditional Anglicans, he joined an association of ministers around Kettering. His passion for unsaved people around the world was evident, though the Kettering group had trouble catching his vision. One of them told him he was not a very good preacher and he needed a lot more practice. Another told him that if the Lord had wanted those pagans to know Jesus, the Almighty would have saved them Himself, without Carey's help.

However, in 1792 this group funded Carey's one-way trip to India. (He aimed for Burma, but trouble with the ship forced him to return to England, where his wife—who'd refused to go at first—

had just given birth.) With an infant and other children in tow, the Careys sailed for India a few days later. Carey set the original mold for many missionary traditions followed today. Becoming bivocational, he earned money teaching at an Indian university. He also became a great botanist, having colleagues in several arenas. Unfortunately, his wife had bouts of mental illness, so William carried much of the evangelistic load alone. He cared for her and the children, taking them with him on many evangelistic excursions. On several occasions he was forced to lock his wife in a closet (a common treatment for mental illness in those days) and preach while she screamed obscenities and banged on the door.

Life must have been hard every day for the Careys, in "the pit of hell," as William had called it before he left England. He certainly was not supported completely by those ministers in Kettering who gave the small gift (under fifteen pounds) to pay his way to India. Though they kept in touch with him, they were unable to hold the ropes for him, as they'd promised earlier. Carey, however, was marching to the tune of a different drummer; he was following his Lord to the ends of the earth.

Leadership of One: A Foolish Way?

Today we'd say he acted foolishly (words his critics may have stated in 1792), but Carey changed his world by accepting a leadership-of-one mentality, launching the modern missionary movement with a majority of one. Realizing his danger in strange places, sorrowful for the sacrifice of his family, but willing to give all for Christ, he accepted responsibility for the gospel, which is "a stumbling block to Jews and foolishness to Gentiles, but to those whom God has called, both Jews and Greeks, Christ the power of God and the wisdom of God. For the foolishness of God is wiser than man's wisdom, and the weakness of God is stronger than man's strength" (1 Corinthians 1:23–25).

Here's a most remarkable irony: from the very beginning, God ignored the world's wisdom. He chose to put His most-cherished treasure into a helpless baby in a manger. The Incarnate Jesus, His only begotten Son, began a worldwide revolution with 12 poor, uneducated men. Paul says, "We have this treasure in jars of clay" (2 Corinthians 4:7). *God had neither a five-year plan in a Disciple Instruction Manual nor a corporate map to show worldwide-marketing progress,* but in 300 years, through the Holy Spirit, the whole Roman Empire was declared Christian!

The Mind-set of a Leadership of One

In 2 Corinthians, Paul had quite a bit to say about the mind-set of a leadership of one. Because of the hope Jesus gives, maturing Christians become "very bold" (3:12). Even though you may feel weak, your iron-will mind-set focuses on the strength you have through Jesus's power. "But he said to me, 'My grace is sufficient for you, for my power is made perfect in weakness'" (12:9). Paul says you are *a letter of recommendation* "written not with ink but with the Spirit of the living God, not on tablets of stone but on tablets of human hearts" (3:3). These words call you to bold witnessing, as you recommend Him to others with confidence. "Such confidence as this is ours though Christ before God.... Our competence comes from God" (3:4–5).

You won't ever be bored as a maturing Christian, because—as He equips you—God will initiate new ministries for you daily. "He has made us competent as ministers of a new covenant" (3:6). The Morningside Baptist Church newsletter (Spartanburg, South Carolina) reflects our church's leadership mind-set. Under a contact roster, it lists "Ministers: All Members of the Congregation." Underneath are the pastors and church staff. Laity lead the list, so each of us can administer the leadership of one, outwardly diminishing in our fleshly importance, but flourishing in our inner spirit.

As a maturing Christian, you don't lose heart. Paul says, "Though outwardly we are wasting away, yet inwardly we are being renewed day by day. For our light and momentary troubles are achieving for us an eternal glory that far outweighs them all" (4:16–17). If you accept it, this is the mind-set of your leadership of one: competent thinking, an optimistic attitude, buoyancy of spirit, joy on your journey, and a labor of love.

List some traits of a leader's mind-set, according to 2 Corinthians:

How would you rate yourself on each of these traits?

The Survival of a Leadership of One

One of the most paradoxical texts in the Bible is this: "For Christ's sake, I delight in weaknesses, in insults, in hardships, in persecutions, in difficulties. For when I am weak, then I am strong" (2 Corinthians 12: 10). Can you imagine Paul saying he delights in insults? You probably would never speak those words! Yet, as you grow in intimacy with the Savior, you find you do more and more things for Him. In this same letter to the church of God in Corinth, Paul says he had asked God to take away a certain "thorn in [his] flesh" (12:7). Scholars have speculated it was a physical defect or handicap; a mental problem, like depression; or even, facetiously, an unfaithful, nagging wife! Whatever it was, it caused suffering in Paul, and God chose *not* to remove it. Remember that Paul writes these words from prison in Rome. Yet in spite of suffering and persecution, the Church of Christ had moved forward phenomenally: "We are hard pressed on every side, but not crushed; perplexed, but not in despair; persecuted, but not abandoned; struck down, but not destroyed" (4:8–9). I've heard many times, "You can't keep a good man (or woman) down." This maxim applies to maturing Christians: you always seek to grow *deeper* in Him, but not feel *down*. Knocked down, but not knocked out. Surviving, yet without a survivor mentality; a victor, not a victim!

Read Hebrews 11:36–40. List the ways Christians suffered persecution:

Do you know people who have been physically, emotionally, or socially persecuted for their faith? Describe the type of persecution they underwent.

Have you ever been shunned or ostracized because of your faith?

Explain your attitude when you are persecuted:

What are you doing to be a target for persecution? (If your answer is "Nothing," then consider whether your faith is even known to those around you.)

List ways you can show your faith this week:

The Reason for a Leadership of One

The usual answer to the question "Why were you created?" is "To glorify God." When Christians, as weak as we are, as immature as we are, accept responsibility for the evangelism of our home, our neighborhood, our country, and our world—one concentric circle at a time—then we're a leadership of one. We've no other desire than to serve God and to yield to Him, sold out to Him in whatever way He wants to use us. *We don't mind being weak, because we want "to show that this all-surpassing power is from God and not from us"* (2 Corinthians 4:7, italics added). That premise is our *raison d'etre*, our reason for being. God says:

> *Think of what you were when you were called. Not many of you were wise by human standards; not many were influential.... But God chose the foolish things of the world to shame the wise; God chose the weak things of the world to shame the strong. He chose the lowly things of this world and the despised things,...so that no one may boast before him. It is*

because of him that you are in Christ Jesus, who has become for us wisdom from God—that is, our right-eousness, holiness and redemption. Therefore, as it is written: "Let him who boasts boast in the Lord." (1 Corinthians 1:26–31)

Let's do that now. Just boast in the Lord and glorify God!

The Challenge of a Leadership of One

In 2001, I received these email statistics: In America, 200 million people work. Since 100 million work for the government (federal, state, county, municipal), that leaves 100 million to do the other work. Of that number, 10 million are in hospitals, leaving 90 million. Some 50 million are in jail or prison, and 39,998,998 are overseas (in the army/business abroad). Of the 1,002 left to do work, 1,000 are in a coma at work. Two people are left to do the work of our nation. However, five minutes before quitting time, a resurrection from the dead occurs, bringing hope for the future.

This is a ridiculous illustration, but it shows the lack of responsibility in the workforce. This lack is minor compared with the lack of responsibility in the *Christian* workforce. If Christianity is to permeate all human hearts, you must toss everything else aside and yield your plan to God's. You must say, like Paul, "I believed; therefore I have spoken" (2 Corinthians 4:13*a*). If you believe Jesus is your Savior, "with that same spirit of faith we also believe and therefore speak" (13*b*). *If you believe it, shout it to the world—even if you're the only one shouting!*

The Direction for a Leadership of One

So where do you go from here? You find direction from God's Word. He is your trainer, leader, and teacher. From Him you gain the following:

- *Righteousness*: "Lead me, O LORD, in your righteousness" (Psalm 5:8).
- *Truth* and *hope*: "Show me your ways, O LORD, teach me your paths; guide me in your truth.... My hope is in you all day long" (Psalm 25:4–5).
- *Optimistic perspective*: "Lead me to the rock that is higher than I" (Psalm 61:2).
- *Avoidance of sin*: "Lead us not into temptation" (Luke 11:4).
- *An innocent heart*: "A little child will lead them" (Isaiah 11:6).

As you mature in the leadership of one, focus on His name: "For the sake of your name lead and guide me" (Psalm 31:3). You may find yourself mumbling, "Only for You, Jesus. Only for You."

However He leads you, ignore distractions, fixing your eyes on Jesus (2 Corinthians 4:18), and the path will be straight. "Teach me your way, O LORD, lead me in a straight path" (Psalm 27:11). He leads, and you become a leadership of one.

M&M: *Ministry and Missions Moment*

William Carey's determination was astounding. He willingly left home, work, church, and friends, marching step by step, listening only to God. He sought, as you do, God's wisdom, not that of the world. Ironically, Carey changed the world by his willingness to go and serve. Though Carey had little of the world's wealth, he was rich in understanding, determination, and courage. As you say, "Only for You, Jesus; only for You," what kind of ministry is God calling you to today? Muster your iron-will determination and move out!

Deeper Still: *Mystery Revealed*

In this book, we've explored ideas on being a blessing for God and others. Many people, like William Carey, have been a blessing for the world, which is better because of their choices. As you pray today, think of this mystery: *You are a leadership influence, one way or another: you can be a curse, a blessing, or a big zero; the choice is yours.*

—— Study 30 ——
When to Stop

You may be one of those maturing Christians who don't know when to stop. You say yes to every ministry and every prayer opportunity. You love the Lord with all your heart and soul and mind and strength. Eagerness and enthusiasm for service is a good mind-set, but sometimes maturing Christians may engage in frantic activity into which God didn't lead them. Sometimes He stops us and *petrifies* us; that is, He ceases all our activity and gives us time to crystallize.

Becoming Petrified

Sue Carver and her mother, Juanita, went to the Petrified Forest. They found themselves staring with amazement and wonder. A precise thinker, Sue says, "The following analogy may cause heartburn for theologians…but the comparison [of petrified trees to mature Christians' lives] has caused me to appreciate one more lesson from nature that reveals the magnificent God we choose to worship before we fully understand the completeness of His intention from the beginning of time." A National Forestry Service guide explained the following:

1. Mighty trees that once stood tall in an impressive forest experienced ever-changing events of time. Some died. Some encountered forces of nature stronger than they—wind and water—that abruptly knocked them down, ending the life they had known.

2. Rivers carried the fallen trees to various places; some were buried in sediment. Volcanoes erupted and ash mixed with the sediment. Ground water dissolved the silica from the ash and carried it through the logs.

3. The silica solution filled and sometimes replaced the trees' cells. The result was beautiful quartz crystals embedded in the preserved details of the log's original surfaces. The quartz combined with other minerals and filled the cracks of the logs, producing beautiful multicolored gems: quartz, purple amethyst, and yellow citrine.

4. Time continues to change their appearance: a shift in the ground causes the logs to fracture, but their brilliance can still be seen in the fragments.

5. Enterprising individuals have stolen some pieces, and others remain in their natural setting. Wherever the pieces reside, they cause those who pass by to pause and marvel.

Here's how our lives as Christians relate to these five stages:

1. Through no decision of ours, we are "planted," born into a specific time and environment. We are what we were designed to be. In life, we make choices that seem right for survival. Then we encounter forces too strong for us to overpower. Car wrecks happen. Cancer happens. Economic hardship happens. And, as a bonus for humans, conscience happens. Not only do we contend with the physical laws of nature, but also the volitional part of us must make a decision regarding our Creator. Through some unique set of events that makes us keenly aware God exists, we're faced with the dilemma of how to respond. Our choice will alter our fate forever.

2. When we allow ourselves to give up what we once were, as a tree falls, we die to our old self. The journey becomes one of unknown destination when we request and accept the new life offered us by our Creator. When His Son made the ultimate sacrifice by accepting *our death destiny* and giving us the option to accept *His life inheritance*, the world experienced a "volcanic eruption." For those who allow Him, He mixes the "ash" from the sacrifice with our "environment's sediments." *His life flows in us.*

3. His Spirit permeates our cells; transformation begins. *The more areas we allow to be exposed to His influence, the more we become like Him.* Through His workmanship, we take on His characteristics. Our attributes remain. We're still recognizable as the outer "tree," as we started, but inside He deposits in us unique gems that reflect various colors of His nature. "I no longer live, but Christ lives in me" (Galatians 2:20).

4. Our appearance changes as the time of day revolves, giving different passersby various perspectives of us. Life's events may change our size and shape, but our core remains constant. Paul says, "Christ in you, the hope of glory" (Colossians 1:27).

5. Regardless of where we reside and what has altered our location, the unusual appearance of our core will cause others to look, pause to understand the transformation, and marvel. *Telling our story reveals the mystery.*

Practice being petrified today. Take a pencil and paper to a quiet place. Sit in silence before God. (You'll remember many errands

or housekeeping jobs on your to-do list. Set them aside.) Once your mind becomes clear, write down anything God tells you:

Write your reactions and actions in response to what you heard God say:

Knowing When to Stop

Many Bible figures knew when to slow down, hush activity, and stop. When the widow Naomi told her two daughters-in-law, Orpah and Ruth (also widows), to go back home to their mothers, Orpah left, but Ruth decided to stick by Naomi. Though Ruth's decision meant Naomi would be responsible for Ruth for the rest of her life, Naomi knew when to quit urging Ruth to go home. Naomi rearranged her life to accommodate Ruth, taking her back to Bethlehem, Naomi's hometown. Her decision to stop asking Ruth to go home was providential: Ruth became the great-grandmother of King David.

One thing I admire about Naomi is that she knew when to stop.

God says there's "a time to search and a time to give up" (Ecclesiastes 3:6). God sometimes provides conditions under which you should *not* witness, volunteer, or serve. Consider the following list of **things to stop**:

1. Your mouth. Sometimes Christians should listen and not talk. Titus 1:10–11 mentions people "whose mouths must be stopped" (KJV). As a maturing Christian, you'll know when you've said enough or too much. The wise action then is to remain silent, to pray in your prayer closet, or to serve as a silent example every day. The psalmist also says, "All iniquity shall stop her mouth" (Psalm 107:42 KJV). When your mouth is about to say anything that will disgrace the name "Christian," just stop.

2. False prophets. Jesus said, "Watch out for false prophets. They come to you in sheep's clothing, but inwardly they are ferocious wolves. By their fruit you will recognize them" (Matthew 7:15–16). At times in your maturation process, you can speak a wise word at the proper time, to prevent false prophets or false doctrines that take away Christian freedoms. Live so that you know when to keep silent, but also when to be courageous in your defense of truth.

3. Evil. God says, "I looked for a man among them who would build up the wall and stand before me in the gap on behalf of the land" (Ezekiel 22:30). God constantly seeks Christians who will stand in the gap to stop the forces of evil. (See also Nehemiah 4.)

4. Hesitation. Unlike the other people who passed by, the good Samaritan (Luke 10:30–37) stopped hesitating and helped the beaten Jew. When God provides a parenthesis in your life (see study 27), stop hesitating and do what is needed.

5. The distortion of truth. "Keep watch over yourselves and all the flock of which the Holy Spirit has made you overseers. Be shepherds of the church of God, which he bought with his own blood. I know that after I leave, savage wolves will come in among you and will not spare the flock. Even from your own number men will arise and distort the truth in order to draw away disciples after them. So be on your guard!" (Acts 20:28–31). Paul gives good advice. Beware of untruthful people.

6. Lingering in bad places. Jesus said, "If anyone will not welcome you or listen to your words, shake the dust off your feet when you leave that home or town.... Therefore be as shrewd as snakes and as innocent as doves" (Matthew 10:14, 16). As you mature, you'll grow a sense of caution and discretion as the Holy Spirit tells you when to quit and leave.

7. Exploiting people and situations. Maturing Christians often find temptation to exploit others or take advantage of unfair situations for their good. When an earthquake broke the shackles and doors on their prison room, the apostles could have taken advantage of the situation (Acts 16:16–36). But they prevented the suicide of the guard and were willing to return to incarceration. When you stop unselfishness in yourself for the good of another, you bring glory to the cause of Christ.

8. Witnessing and ministry, under special conditions. Like this book, even the best ministries have a natural time of ending. Make sure your work for the Lord is directed by Him. If it's not, stop. Throughout Acts, you will find examples of times the early apostles quit a ministry. When they were endangering the local people, when they were causing too much controversy, when God called them to another place of service, and when staying would cause a negative influence for Christianity, they moved on. When they felt God leading, they were willing to risk all, rejoicing in being flogged or imprisoned for their faith, but under some circumstances, they peacefully left town.

Shakespeare said, "Discretion is the better part of valor." This principle holds true for Christians, as God leads.

Write examples of times when you thought you needed to stop each of the eight listed *things to stop*.

1.

2.

3.

4.

5.

6.

7.

8.

Rhinestones Don't Make a Cowboy

"Dub" Chambers, author of the Beehive Evangelism materials (see www.beehiveevangelism.com), had a repetitive dream of someone asking him to wear a cowboy shirt with gold rhinestones all over it. He insisted that wearing that shirt would not make him an authentic cowboy. Growing up in Las Animas, Colorado, he had worked around animals, and his two uncles were real cowboys. In his dream, he ridiculously kept shouting at the gift giver: "Rhinestones don't make a cowboy. If you ever meet a real cowboy, you'll know the difference." The giver asked, "What's the difference between a rhinestone Christian and a real one?" At this point, Dub awakened, but for several days he pondered that question, applying it to the church he pastors, but especially applying it to his own life. He says, "I'm convinced we are nothing but rhinestone Christians unless we let Jesus do a deep and vast work within the core of our inner being."

Being Complete

This book began with the concept of holiness. Jesus said, "Be perfect, therefore, as your heavenly Father is perfect" (Matthew 5:48). The Greek word for *perfect* in this verse is *teleos*, or *complete*, translated, "Be complete as your Father is complete." As you grow deeper as a maturing Christian, you will become more complete in every way. Finding spiritual maturity is not a quick process. As you have studied this book, you have only scratched the surface. Hours of *delving into the deep* await you. Kirk Neely says: "It takes a lifetime. We don't reach spiritual maturity until our lives are almost over, if ever."

At the end of His life on earth, Jesus said, "It is finished" (John 19:30). He had completed His mission on earth that day, but His Holy Spirit will continue to refine your heart. As your study of this book is complete, my prayer is that you'll invite Him into all the deep recesses of your heart and that He'll continue to pour His Spirit into you.

Of all the unit studies you've completed in this book, which ones were the most significant?

How has God spoken to you, leading you deeper and deeper still?

M&M: *Ministry and Missions Moment*

Although you are *born again* when you accept Jesus into your heart, you **never stop** the quest for intimacy with Him. He will continue to refine you, making you truly an authentic Christian. *Don't be a rhinestone Christian.* Be yourself. Keep the lines of communication open, without a flashy outer shell or barrier. You can tell God anything; He never condemns. "There is no condemnation for those who are in Christ Jesus" (Romans 8:1). "The gift of God is eternal life in Christ Jesus our Lord" (Romans 6:23). Celebrate your authentic gift of eternal life and communicate it to others!

Deeper Still: Mystery Revealed

To be petrified is to die to your old self and allow the supernatural influx of God's Spirit into your being. As Sue Carver says, "If we can see the jewels in the description [of the Holy City in Revelation 21:14–20] as representing us in our Christ-filled, ultimately perfected state, then we must be petrified by Christ, captured by Him. Today we marvel at the miracle God performed in us when we accepted His offer to be eternally 'petrified' with his precious Jewel—the Holy Spirit."

As a maturing Christian, you have an inner sparkle like the petrified trees in the forest. *God never stops sparkling in you. The more you allow Him to indwell who you are, the more of Him others see in you.* Be faithful to the sparkle. Jesus said if people like you who have witnessed the miracles of God keep silent, "the stones will cry out" (Luke 19:40)! Meditate today on this mystery.

To God be the glory, great things He has done!

OTHER FAITH-BUILDING STUDIES

Friend to Friend: *Enriching Friendships Through a Shared Study of Philippians*
By Edna Ellison
ISBN 1-56309-710-9

Friendships of Faith: *A Shared Study of Hebrews*
By Edna Ellison
ISBN 1-56309-762-1

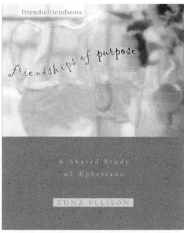

Friendships of Purpose: *A Shared Study of Ephesians*
By Edna Ellison
ISBN 1-56309-901-2

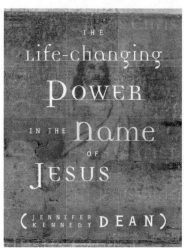

The Life-Changing Power in the Name of Jesus
By Jennifer Kennedy Dean
ISBN 1-56309-841-5

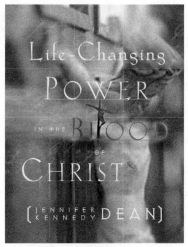

The Life-Changing Power in the Blood of Christ
By Jennifer Kennedy Dean
ISBN 1-56309-753-2

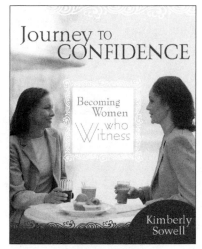

Journey to Confidence:
Becoming Women Who Witness
By Kimberly Sowell
ISBN 1-56309-923-3

new
hope
PUBLISHERS

Available in bookstores everywhere

For information about these books or any New Hope products, visit www.newhopepublishers.com.

New Hope® Publishers is a division of WMU®,
an international organization that challenges Christian believers
to understand and be radically involved in God's mission.
For more information about WMU, go to www.wmu.com.
More information about New Hope books may be found
at www.newhopepublishers.com. New Hope books
may be purchased at your local bookstore.